THE LITTLE BOOK OF

W0013610

THE END OF THE WORLD

KEN MOONEY

ILLUSTRATED BY SARAH CUNNINGHAM

The
History
Press

First published 2014

The History Press
The Mill, Brimscombe Port
Stroud, Gloucestershire, GL5 2QG
www.thehistorypress.co.uk

British Library Cataloguing in Publication Data.
A catalogue record for this book is available from the British Library.

ISBN 978 0 7509 5641 3

Typesetting and origination by The History Press
Printed in Great Britain

CONTENTS

ACKNOWLEDGEMENTS

I probably won't remember to thank all of the people who helped to make this book possible: there are a lot of them, and even if you didn't make it to this page, you still deserve my thanks. So to everyone who's known about this project and offered your help, support and kind words – thank you.

My family, who gave me everything I ever needed: like most families, I probably didn't realise that until many years later.

Dan – at some stage, you won't need to keep telling me you believe in me, and I might believe you. But that's not an excuse to stop.

Sarah Cunningham – your illustrations have brought to life some crazy ideas and weird concepts that I thought were confined to my head. Working together has been amazing, and I'm looking forward to doing it again. And thanks to Sean Redahan for suggesting we do it.

Declan Flynn and the rest of the gang at THP – thanks for believing in this little book, and in my ability to make it happen.

Kiera Bruce, Michael Neville, Tim Nagle and anyone else I've asked random questions of: now you know why.

Dave and John Hendrick, Bruno Batista and everyone else involved in DICE, without whom I'd never have the pep-talks and confidence to do this stuff.

Claire C. Riley, Adam Oster, Eli Constant and Wulf Francu Goldgluck – I met a crazy bunch of people all embarking on a weird literary journey at around the same time. You've provided some great company and friendship, and I wouldn't trade it for anything.

INTRODUCTION

This is a book about the End of the World: consider yourself warned.

It's not a simple thing to write a book about. After all, the world is a big place and there are many, many ways in which it could come to an end. In fact, there are probably more world-ending events that could happen than we could fit into a book this size and still call it 'little'. This book addresses just some of them.

As a species, we think about the End of the World a lot: we talk about it, we write about it, we worry about it. We even make plans for what we'd do if and when it happens.

The End of the World captures our imagination with fantastical imagery of fire and brimstone, of gigantic monsters and the dead returning to life. But it also reminds us of our own mortality, posing one massive question: what will we do when faced with our imminent death?

The End of the World affects us both on a personal level and as a much larger culture as well: whole religions and philosophies have developed, some taking their fear and thoughts about the End of the World as a starting point, others suggesting that salvation is possible, and that those faithful few will not be affected by the End. These religions don't just have their ideas about how the world will end, but what we, as individuals, should do to ensure that we'll survive when it happens.

But the End isn't always the End: even in the face of war and destruction, we're an optimistic bunch, and we have convinced ourselves that there might be something coming afterwards, that maybe if this world ends, there's another world that will have us.

Waiting for the End has overshadowed whole lives and cultures, even started wars. While the End of the World might bring us together as a people, there are so many different ideas about it that these ideas divide us as well.

The End of the World is no laughing matter. Until you've lived through it, and then it becomes something you can joke about over a few drinks.

In fact, in addition to all these theories about how the world will end, we've all survived multiple near misses, becoming hardened survivalists, and earning the right to be flippant about the Apocalypse. After all, the Mayans had us all written off by 2012; the computers – or perhaps it was the computer programmers – were coming to get us for Y2K; and let's not forget the mad scientists in their underground bunkers who threatened to wipe us out to recreate the Big Bang. That's three averted high-profile Apocalypses in just twelve years.

In this book, we'll look at those near misses that fill us with confidence, as well as the beliefs that drive our fears.

First, we'll talk about some of the real threats that our home planet throws our way, wiping out small communities and leaving us with horror stories that have instilled fear in our ancestors. Some of these fears turned into legitimate beliefs, and there are many religious elements to the End of the World: we'll look at how our collective faith, hopes and fears have influenced our thoughts about the Endtimes.

Finally, we'll also look at some specific cases, near misses or moments from the world of politics that have hit especially close to home: perhaps somebody thought the world would end, but it didn't; or maybe somebody did something crazy or stupid, forever changing how we think about the End of the World.

Don't let that scare you. We've lived through it all.

If that doesn't make you feel invincible, nothing will.

THE LANGUAGE
OF THE
END OF THE WORLD

There are as many different ways of talking about the End of the World as there are theories how it might happen. Some are conversations to be spoken in the whispered tones of fear – just in case the alien overlords overhear; others are discussed with the religious fervour of someone assured that they are among the righteous who will be saved.

For the purposes of this book, we'll be using the lot of them, sometimes even in the right context!

The guide below should give you an idea of some of their origins, and why certain words or phrases are used hand-in-hand with the End of the World.

The End of the World – In case you're unsure what a book about the End of the World will be discussing, we're looking at the end of civilisation or the destruction of our home planet, whichever comes first and however that might happen.

As civilisation has grown and changed, so too has the idea of the End of the World: for older cultures, unaware of the size or scope of the planet, the End of the World might have been as small as the elimination of their own town or village, and this book will look at some smaller acts of destruction as well as those larger ones.

Endtimes/End of Days – There are several different words used throughout religious movements to talk about the End of the World: the Endtimes and End of Days are just two of them. These are used almost exclusively in a religious context, implying that time and humanity will be brought to an end, rather than the world itself. While these Endtimes are typically Christian, there are many similarities between Christianity and other world religions.

Eschatology – A Greek word where the 'ch' is pronounced like a 'k', eschatology is the study of the Endtimes: this could be an academic comparison of all religions or a catch-all word to describe everything associated with the End of the World in one religion – so 'Christian eschatology' refers to all thoughts and beliefs associated with the Endtimes of that particular religion.

Eschatology is not exclusively religious, however: modern studies have started to incorporate politics and technology into discussions about the End of the World, treating them as equally important as the religious elements.

By picking up this book, you've just confirmed yourself as an amateur eschatologist.

Apocalypse – One of the words most widely used to describe and discuss the End of the World, 'apocalypse' is also the least appropriate.

'Apocalypse' is a Greek word meaning 'removing a veil' and is used to mean the realisation of knowledge: it is used interchangeably with 'Revelations' as the name for the last book of the Bible. In this book, the writer outlines a dream about the End of the World and discusses the knowledge he gets from witnessing these events: it is an Apocalyptic dream because of this realisation, not because of the events of the dream.

Armageddon – Derived from religious references to the End of the World across Christian, Jewish and Muslim beliefs, Armageddon specifically refers to the place where a great battle between good and evil will happen.

The name is mentioned in the Bible and could come from 'Har Megiddo' or 'the hill of Megiddo', an actual location in modern Israel.

Dystopia – Dystopia is a word that's proven very popular in recent years, especially in a fictional context. If utopia is a paradise then dystopia is its natural opposite, a place marked by corrupt governments, starvation and other dangers.

This dystopian world goes hand-in-hand with the post-Apocalyptic world, as writers and philosophers ponder how civilisation will respond to an End of the World that still leaves some of us alive and present on the Earth.

Unfortunately, there have been a few occasions in human history that have given us a good idea of what could happen if this came to pass.

PART 1

THE ANGRY EARTH

It's very easy to be confident in the face of the Apocalypse – until we remember what this planet has already been through.

As a species, modern humans have only been occupying this rock for the last 200,000 years. On a planet that is approximately 4.5 billion years old, that makes us a tiny blip on the radar. For the mathematically minded amongst you, our occupancy of the Earth barely amounts to a couple of thousandths of one per cent of time. In the great intergalactic court of natural order, we probably wouldn't even have a case to argue for squatters' rights.

During our tenancy, there are many things that the Earth has thrown at us: we call them 'natural disasters' because of the effects they have on civilisation, but they're pretty standard parts of the planet's life cycle.

1

PLANET-KILLERS AND CREATORS

Most of what the planet throws our way does a lot more damage to humans and man-made structures than to the face of the Earth. For humans, a 'natural disaster' may cause the loss of life or limb, but to the planet such events are more like a minor case of acne.

But before we look at some of these internal threats, we should look at the bigger picture: what about those that come from outside? Like the neighbours' bratty kids, the universe has a tendency to throw rocks at our windows. Even as mankind looks to the sky with aspirations and promises of success, there are still things up there just waiting for their opportunity to fall on us.

ASTEROIDS, METEORS AND COMETS: WHAT'S THE DIFFERENCE?

Like terms about the End of the World itself, the above three words get used almost interchangeably, but there are some very specific differences. Of course, nobody really argues semantics when a giant ball of rock is flying at their planet.

Asteroids

These are the dangerous ones, but there isn't much reason to worry: most of the asteroids we know about come nowhere near the Earth.

Most of them.

Asteroids are planetoids, chunks of rock and metal that float around our solar system: some formed on their own, while others are the debris left over after small planets or other celestial bodies have broken up.

Most of the asteroids in our solar system are located between Mars and Jupiter, suggesting that, at some stage, there were other planets or large bodies occupying this space. This was a common view amongst nineteenth-century astronomers, but later discoveries have challenged those opinions: these asteroids are made up of different minerals and rocks, too dissimilar to have a common origin.

There are several million asteroids in this asteroid belt, with anywhere up to 2 million of them a whopping kilometre in diameter. If you've ever dropped a bowling ball – average diameter of 21cm – you should have an idea of the destruction any asteroid impact could cause to planet Earth.

The sheer distance from these asteroids means that an impact from any of them is unlikely to ever happen. However, there are other asteroids loitering around our solar system, just looking for their opportunity to cause some damage: some of these are so close that they're even designated as being 'near-Earth'.

NASA has estimated that there are nearly 1,000 of these near-Earth asteroids – if there is any immediate danger to our planet, it will come from these. Both the Aten and Apollo asteroid ranges have sent visitors our way recently, and if something even bigger comes, it would have its origin here.

Meteors

Meteoroids are significantly smaller than asteroids, up to a metre in diameter, making them about the size of a Mini Cooper.

Size is the only real difference between an asteroid and a meteor: in fact, they're likely to have the same origins, with most meteors formed from the debris of asteroids. Some meteors could have their origins closer to home, however, with some formed by rubble from a prehistoric Earth or the moon.

There's a precise science to naming meteors too:

♦ the piece of rock in space (or entering the Earth's atmosphere) is referred to as a meteoroid;
♦ as the meteoroid enters the atmosphere, it will start to break up, forming a meteor. This word specifically refers to the blazing trail left by the meteoroid, not the piece of rock;
♦ when what is left of the meteoroid has burnt up and reacted with the Earth's atmosphere, the metallic rock that strikes the Earth is known as a meteorite.

Comets

Like a meteoroid, a comet is a small body, but it is not formed of rocks and minerals: instead, a comet is formed from ice and dust, with the visible effects of the comet's tail caused by the reflection and refraction of light as the comet flies through space.

Comets typically have an orbit, either around the sun or another celestial body: that means that their appearance can be predicted, and most of the comets that we see today have visited before. It also means that impacts are very unlikely, with comets and our home planet having partaken in this complicated dance for millions of years.

However, small changes to the orbit of a comet can take place, so comets can still end up moving closer – or further away – on successive passes. Halley's Comet in particular has caused numerous scares involving potential impacts, usually caused by predictions made about what the comet could bring with it.

ROCKS IN SPACE AND THE END OF THE WORLD

With all those rocks floating around our planet, it's little wonder that there are so many opportunities for collisions: it's not just the concern of movies like 1998's inappropriately titled *Armageddon*.

In fact, there are plenty of collisions that never quite make it to the evening news. These are typically called 'impact events', but don't always involve an impact: in many cases, a meteoroid or other body will burn up as it enters Earth's atmosphere, turning an impact event into a non-event.

But don't get too confident.

There have been noteworthy impact events in the past that might have changed the shape and future of this planet. Who knows what could happen if another one like these occurred?

The Moon's Secret Origins?

Back 4.5 billion years ago, the Earth was just a toddler. And like every foundling child, the planet was prone to a few bumps and scrapes.

A number of scientists have put forward a theory that the moon was created after a 'giant impact event' but this would have had to be with the mother of all asteroids: the current theory is that this impact was with something the size and density of Mars.

This doesn't mean that this impact created a moon-sized crater that we've somehow not noticed over the last few millennia: at this stage of the Earth's formation, the planet would not have been fully solid, and the impact would have kicked up significant amounts of the material that would soon form the surface of the planet. As this matter cooled and recovered, there would have been enough gravitational forces at work to force things back into a spherical shape.

Tests carried out on samples from the lunar surface have made this a pretty likely suggestion for the moon's origin: our planet's only satellite is made from very similar materials to the planet itself, but is curiously lacking in some of the minerals that are found closer to the Earth's core. In other words, if the moon was formed by the galactic equivalent of an organ donation, it was done with surface material.

What Killed the Dinosaurs?

Sixty-six million years ago, dinosaurs ruled the Earth. That's what Richard Attenborough told us in *Jurassic Park*, and I won't hear it any other way.

In reality, there was plenty of other life roaming our planet around then, and scientists have found proof of insects, lizards, birds and fish that aren't too dissimilar from the animals that are still alive today.

So why don't we see any dinosuars?

The notions of an asteroid killing the dinosaurs creates visions of a massive impact, with the dinosaurs dying rapidly in the following shockwaves, but what likely happened was a little bit slower and a lot less dramatic: any impact would have raised a massive dust cloud that killed off most of the plant life and had lasting effects up the food chain.

Proof of this brings us all the way to Mexico and a place called Chicxulub: the area's interesting topography means this could have been the site of a massive impact event, and geological studies done in the 1970s appear to confirm just that. In a massive coincidence, this impact would have occurred around 66 million years ago. While this wouldn't have killed off all the dinosaurs in one go, and some species would have survived a little longer than that, the timing is too close to be a coincidence.

Brace yourself for the figures: the Chicxulub crater is about 180km wide and was probably caused by an asteroid nearly 10km in diameter. That's about the size of New York's Central Park.

30 June 1908: Tunguska, Russia

A streak of blue light moves across the sky near the Tunguska River, followed by an explosion that smashes windows, knocks people off their feet and flattens 2,000sq.km of woodland.

Even a century later, the Tunguska event courts the attention of conspiracy theorists, in no small part due to the closed borders and secrecy of different Russian regimes throughout the twentieth century. But various studies have been carried out in the area, all of which agree that the site saw some form of impact event, but leaving scientists nonplussed by the lack of an obvious crater.

So when is an impact event not an impact event?

When the asteroid explodes in mid-air with such force that the shockwave is solely responsible for the destruction. It almost sounds too good to be true, had the events not been repeated just over a century later.

15 February 2013: Chelyabinsk, Russia

Russia gets another close call with a collision, this time near the city of Chelyabinsk, only 2,000km away from Tunguska. Once again the celestial body burned up before impact, creating a shockwave that could be seen and felt for miles around, smashing windows and causing considerable destruction.

Like the Tunguska event, there was significant property damage. Unlike Tunguska, the Chelyabinsk event took place in the age of digital media and got caught on camera, with footage and images making their way onto international news networks.

THE PLANET KILLER

With so many impacts and near misses, we have to wonder if it's possible that an impact event on a massive scale could wipe us out. Hollywood would have us believe that it would be a fiery, quick death, but as we've learned from the dinosaurs, it's far more likely that it would be slow and involve a significant lack of food: after all, our dependence on plant life and the bottom of the food chain is no less important to us than it was to the dinosaurs.

As we discover more about the history of the planet on which we're living, we realise it is only a matter of time before an impact event occurs of significant size to create damage to a town or settlement. Whether that would spell the End of the World probably depends on how close you live to this impact.

Could a massive impact truly 'kill' the planet? Probably not.

Could it be the End of the World?

Maybe.

2

THE ELEMENTS AGAINST US: WATER, FIRE, EARTH AND WIND

We humans are pretty sturdy creatures. Well, except for the tendency to break limbs, require a perfectly balanced diet, our general susceptibility to disease, illness, poison, fatal allergies and a tendency to kill each other when we don't get our own way.

Actually, when you think about it, we're quite a picky bunch. It's no wonder that it sometimes seems like the Earth is out to get us.

There are many elements that contribute to the Earth's ecosystem and its perfect balance for supporting human life. The modern world thinks of these elements in atomic terms, with life – as we know it – requiring a careful balance of carbon, hydrogen, oxygen and nitrogen, amongst others, to flourish.

But before mankind became aware of atomic numbers and electron microscopes, most schools of thought accepted that there were four basic elements that formed the world around us: water, fire, earth and wind. These are still referenced in meteorological terms, by fictional superheroes and American funk bands of the 1970s.

With the world around us being made of these classical elements, it should come as no surprise that its inevitable end would involve a significant upset to the balance between all four.

LOCATION, LOCATION, LOCATION: THE PERFECT BALANCE

Life on this planet suffers from something of a Goldilocks complex: it just can't support itself if things are too hot or too cold. This perfect balance operates on both local and global levels: there are extreme temperatures that render some parts of our planet uninhabitable, and if you've ever worked or lived with other people, you probably know the difference that a tiny notch on a dial can make, whether it's the heater or air conditioning.

Earth is at an optimum distance from the sun to support human life, and above all else, keep us comfortable. Our seasons are all relative to the distance from the sun and the axis of the planet at any given time: it's a predictable method of how we know that our winters will be cold and our summers will be warm. Or at least warmer than it is in winter.

This is all such a fragile balance that even a tiny change in the Earth's axis or in the composition of the elements in the air or water would change the climate significantly, potentially making it different enough to wipe humans off the face of the planet.

Climate change has become a talking point since the end of the twentieth century and an urgent action point for many organisations and governments, as any man-made changes to the climate could have disastrous effects on the planet's ability to recover.

It's unlikely that any change would happen overnight, but small changes could still prove cataclysmic to society and human life.

But even without interference from human inhabitants or a colliding celestial body to knock us off course, the Earth can still undergo these changes on its own.

The Ice Age

'The Ice Age' is one of those phrases that rolls off the tongue as if it describes only one period of the planet's history: there have actually been at least five ice ages in the Earth's history – there could even

have been more, but we only have proof of five. The most recent of these ice ages was in the Quaternary or Pleistocene period, which started around 2.5 million years ago.

Any ice age is caused by – and creates – a significant change in the Earth's atmosphere and climate, with the predominant activity during this period creating large sheets of ice that cover a significantly large part of the planet: the Pleistocene ice age led to the creation of the ice sheets that currently form a large part of the Arctic and Antarctic areas of the Earth.

But these ice sheets do not need to cover the entire planet in order to be considered an ice age, nor does it mean that the rest of the Earth is uninhabitable. There were plenty of different life forms which survived or evolved through the last ice age.

If another ice age were to suddenly begin, its progress would be slow enough that we'd have time to migrate in the short term, and over a longer period, evolve to deal with the extreme temperatures. Or at least forego some of our more invasive methods of hair removal.

We also have at least a couple of thousand years to prepare, with the next Big Chill estimated to happen in around 150,000 years. Of course, that could end up being significantly sooner if man-made climate change continues at its current rate.

Water

For a planet covered in so much water and ice, you'd think it wouldn't be as deadly and destructive as it is. But even after all these years, humans still haven't developed gills or a natural way of dealing with the pressures of the ocean's depths.

Drowning isn't the only threat that water carries: the oceans alone have destructive ebbs and flows that cause erosion and flooding, and that's before you consider rivers and rainfall. Flooding, in particular, is becoming an unfortunately regular occurrence around the British Isles, with the after-effects of storms providing something of a post-Apocalyptic vision on the news headlines at least once a year.

But could there ever be a large, powerful flood, strong enough that it would wipe us off the face of the planet?

There are some religious suggestions that such a flood has already happened at least once in history and we'll discuss that a little bit later. However, proof is, understandably, a little difficult to come by

But even amongst the stories of Noah and the various myths of Atlantis and other sunken islands, there are plenty of submerged cities and underwater ruins that lend some proof to these stories, while also bearing witness to the mighty destructive power of water.

Heracleion, Egypt

Be careful with the spelling when you're visiting this ancient city, as you might end up in Heraklion in Crete. Both cities are named after the classical Greek hero and demi-god Hercules, but this city's ruins lie across the Mediterranean in modern Egypt.

Heracleion was a major Egyptian port and centre of trade for nearly 1,500 years until it sank into the sea around the sixth century AD. The city's destruction was blamed on a massive earthquake and the resulting floods that washed over the area, redefining the coastline.

The city's ruins are located in Abu Qir Bay, an area that's also steeped in more-recent history as the site of Nelson's Battle of the Nile.

Despite the proximity of the city of Alexandria, the ruins of the city were lost until the year 2000 when Franck Goddio, a well-known underwater archaeologist, started to investigate the area and discovered that most of Heracleion's statues and artefacts were still immaculately preserved underwater.

Helike, Greece

The Greek god of the sea Poseidon was supposedly responsible for the destruction of Helike in 373 BC, but the chances are it might have just been another earthquake.

Helike was located near the Greek city of Patras. With the city located in a densely populated area, there are many contemporary stories about its destruction: supposedly rats, dogs and cats all fled the city prior to its sinking, and afterwards, the site became a tourist attraction to the locals who navigated their boats around the city's statues and rooftops.

After the seabed settled and Helike's features were lost in sand and silt, the city was subsequently treated as an urban legend until it was rediscovered in 2001.

Villa Epecuén, Argentina

Helike and Heracleion aren't the only cities that have fallen into the sea, but you would think we as a species had learned our lesson and would stop building cities in areas that were prone to flooding, earthquakes or right underneath a big dam that could possibly burst and cause a flood.

But as recently as 1920, that lesson still hadn't sunk in.

Villa Epecuén was a holiday village built near the Atlantic coast of Argentina: the village catered to holidaying citizens from nearby Buenos Aires, somewhat like Butlin's with more sun and better football players.

In 1985, after a season of persistant heavy rains, the man-made Lake Epecuén overflowed, flooding its banks and destroying the dam that had kept the city safe. The water levels have only started to subside in recent years, with Vila Epecuén experiencing a renaissance befitting the twenty-first century, promising visitors a glimpse at a post-Apocalyptic wasteland.

Fire

We've looked at water and ice, so it's only fair that we continue to look at their opposite: fire. Just as water is necessary for drinking and hygiene, we also have an intrinsic need for fire, whether it's to keep us warm, to cook our food or to help us crank up the heat so we can stay up all night binge-watching TV box sets.

Heat in itself is something we all crave, especially with some of the local wet summers of the British Isles, but there are still parts of the planet made uninhabitable by hot and arid conditions. In fact, the various deserts dotted around the planet's surface are just as dangerous as the oceans, with both having equally demanding borders. Like the oceans, these deserts are not devoid of life: the desert has its own unique flora and fauna, and an estimated 40 per cent of the world's population live in or near these arid areas.

Even in the form of molten lava spewing forth from the bowels of the planet, fire is not a wholly destructive element. In fact islands like Hawaii and the Canary Islands have been formed as a result of volcanic eruptions, with land that has proven to be incredibly fertile.

But there's still something incredibly terrifying about volcanoes, conjuring mental images of fleeing from clouds of black ash and rivers of lava; they're almost like something made just to represent the End of the World.

And with good reason.

Pompeii, Italy

The eruption of Mount Vesuvius in AD 79 destroyed the town of Pompeii and nearby Heracleum, about 300km south of Rome.

But contrary to what we might think about volcanoes, Mount Vesuvius didn't actually burn everything to a crisp: instead, the ash preserved buildings and bodies alike until they were rediscovered in 1599.

Much of the organic matter has long since decayed, but archaeologists have started to use plaster and rubber resin to make casts to preserve the shapes of the bodies as they have lain for nearly 2,000 years.

Pompeii has turned into one of those otherworldly locations where tourists can now visit and see a snapshot of life and death side by side.

*Icelandic Volcanoes, or what I
didn't do on my 2010 Summer Holidays*

Volcanoes aren't always a destructive force: they have given us fertile land, like Lanzarote, Samoa and Hawaii that have been formed as a result of a volcanic eruption. These islands have given us summer holidays, wrestlers and shooting locations for TV and movies.

And then there's Iceland.

It's not so much that Iceland is a bad place as it is the location of the most recent large-scale volcanic eruption, and one that is still fresh in our memories.

Eyjafjallajökull erupted multiple times in April 2010, causing no end of heartache to reporters and journalists who had to spell and say the word. It also created an ash cloud that caused widespread disruption to European and transatlantic air travel, which just happened to coincide with many people's spring and summer holidays.

The Door to Hell

In the centre of Turkmenistan lies the imaginatively titled Door to Hell, a terrifying natural feature that is as much a creation of humanity as it is a reminder of the dangerous forces beneath our feet.

In the 1970s, the gas-rich Darvaza region was close to being exploited by Soviet scientists who were ready to use the area's gas supply for fuel. However, during excavation, a sinkhole developed, swallowing the ground and much of the equipment. The project began to leak dangerous methane into the atmosphere, affecting nearby towns. Faced with the decision between expensive repair work and a speedy solution to the imminent environmental crisis, it was decided to set fire to the gas field, burning up both the fuel and the methane and eliminating the problem.

Forty years later, the hole continues to burn, the wide chasm forming a fiery pit that has excited the imagination of many artists. The Door to Hell isn't quite the End of the World, but it sure does look like it.

Earth

The phrase 'solid ground' may be frequently used, but the earth beneath our feet is anything but. As continents and tectonic plates shift in a complicated dance, the civilisations that grow on top of them become unwitting partners which might end up taking a fall if and when the dance floor gets crowded.

There are several different phenomena that can affect the ground beneath our feet, and more than a handful of communities have met their end by landslides, avalanches, sinkholes and earthquakes. Many of these are caused by a combination of elements, with landslides and sinkholes typically caused by water and earth working together in one destructive event.

Landslides vary from a heavy flow of water that will carry earth, trees and buildings along with them, to a light flow of sand and soil particles that have been set off by rains or building work. The most recent large-scale disaster involving a landslide occurred in 2011 in Rio de Janeiro where a series of floods and subsequent mudslides caused at least 900 deaths.

Sinkholes are formed in a similar way, with water causing subterranean layers of earth to erode, causing the topmost layer to collapse. This can be common in urban areas, where building works have further undermined lower layers of earth and rubble, leaving only man-made structures to support concrete streets and sometimes whole buildings.

Earthquakes are caused by the release of energy as tectonic plates shift or collide: they're a regular occurrence, with half a million earthquakes of varying intensity occuring each year. Some are barely felt, while others cause large-scale destruction.

While the nature of earthquakes, and the way they are measured, means they can be predicted and detected around the world, it's unlikely that an earthquake would ever occur of the magnitude and scale that it would bring about an apocalyptic threat to humanity.

But that's not to say that the smaller ones should be ignored.

1755: Lisbon

While most earthquakes and volcanic activity centre on the Pacific Ocean and its neighbouring countries, one of the most deadly earthquakes in recorded history actually took place in the Atlantic Ocean and had devastating effects on the Portuguese capital of Lisbon.

The Lisbon earthquake struck on the morning of 1 November, and is believed to have measured around 8.5 on the Richter scale. The earthquake itself wasn't the sole harbinger of destruction to the city: the quake caused fires and a massive tsunami that washed over the coast.

Up to 100,000 people were killed as a result of the earthquake, with most of the city's structures destroyed.

1906: San Francisco

On 18 April 1906, an earthquake measuring 7.8 struck San Francisco. Estimates suggest that nearly 3,000 people were killed in the quake, but given the city's high immigrant population, many of whom were illegal and not officially recorded, there is no official figure for the death toll.

The earthquake destroyed most of San Francisco, with tremors felt along the Pacific Coast and as far inland as Nevada.

2011: Japan

As if to prove that earthquakes can sometimes be a precursor to much greater destruction, on 11 March 2011, an earthquake struck 70km off the coast of Japan. While Japan is a country used to earthquakes, with an infrastructure designed to withstand most minor quakes, this quake measured 9.0 on the Richter scale and constituted one of the greatest disasters to ever strike the country: over 15,000 people died, and nearly a million buildings were destroyed or damaged by the earthquake or the subsequent flooding.

The 2011 Japanese earthquake is just one example of a megathrust earthquake, with seismologists expecting that there could be another one very soon – this is casually referred to as The Big One by inhabitants of the Western USA and Japan. Megathrust earthquakes typically rank over 8.0 on the Richter scale and are localised to the Pacific Ocean, based on the constant activity between the Philippine Sea Plate and North American Plate.

However, despite the dangers presented by the 2011 earthquake, most of the headlines focused on the damage caused to the Fukushima nuclear plant.

As the earthquake struck, the Fukushima nuclear power plant entered shutdown, in accordance with the plant's safety protocols. However, the following tsunami created problems for the plant, flooding most of the complex and disabling the diesel generators that were providing the plant's safety systems, including coolant for the reactor. This led to a number of small explosions, releasing nuclear material into both the water supply and the air.

All eyes were on Fukushima, expecting an imminent nuclear disaster that never came: the Japanese government claimed

that there were no adverse effects after the Fukushima disaster. However, in 2013 it was revealed that the plant is continuing to leak radioactive water into the Pacific Ocean.

Wind

And finally, we have the last of the classical elements: the mighty wind. While air is always present, we usually have to wait for some act of ultimate devastation to be reminded of its destructive power.

Like water, earth and fire, wind is not a solely destructive force: it can be used to generate electricity or dry clothes. But its unpredictable nature makes the wind even more dangerous than the other elements.

The greatest act of the angry wind is the hurricane, also known as the tropical storm, typhoon or cyclone – the phrasing usually depends on what area you're living in. This type of storm is caused by evaporating water from the ocean's surface which rapidly cools and forms clouds. The quick heating and cooling of this water builds up significant amounts of energy which combines with an initial low pressure to form a tropical storm.

2005: Hurricane Katrina

On 23 August 2005, Hurricane Katrina began to form in the middle of the Atlantic Ocean, making landfall on 25 August. The hurricane swept through Florida, Louisiana and Mississippi, later changing course and joining with another storm front to affect areas as far north as Quebec.

Hurricane Katrina caused nearly 2,000 deaths and several billion dollars of structural damage.

The hurricane's effects are still felt in the city of New Orleans, where over 80 per cent of the city was flooded, destroying homes and businesses. The city still hasn't fully recovered. Hurricane Katrina remains one of the most costly natural disasters to ever strike the United States, both in terms of property damage and lives lost.

PART 2

RELIGIONS OF THE WORLD

The Earth beneath our feet is out to get us, with the universe throwing all sorts of obstacles in our way, like a comic-book supervillain.

It should come as no surprise that most of our myths and legends about the beginning and end of the world revolve around these treacherous forces.

The earliest religions are built around these natural forces, with cultures giving names and identities to the actions of the Earth that they didn't understand. These became the early pagan gods, developing personalities that brought them into conflict with each other. The gods became the heart of long and complicated stories that incorporated the wealth of human experience and tried to explain the mysteries of the world around us.

Despite the fact that these mythologies and religions flourished independently around the globe, there are surprisingly common elements to all, terrifying similarities between the forces that we once believed would destroy us and the methods in which we thought the end would come.

3

CLASSICAL RELIGIONS AND THE FAMILIES OF GODS

Most of the religions that are widely practised in the twenty-first century are built on a monotheistic structure, the belief in one god or 'supreme being'; that god is responsible for our creation, for the creation of the world around us and, ultimately, whatever end we might meet.

The classical world had some pretty similar beliefs, but there was no single god: instead, we were given a family, or pantheon of gods. Each element of the world was attributed to a different god or spirit, all with complex interpersonal relationships. Under these gods, thunderstorms weren't just an act of god but an epic battle for supremacy in the heavens, with flooding and other destructive acts sent as divine punishment for humanity.

The presence of the gods made sense of an illogical world, explaining the cyclical nature of the Earth, its days and its seasons. But the gods also helped to make sense of life itself: heroes and kings were created as the gods intervened in their lives, favouring them over all others; families were destroyed as their prideful actions sought to rival the glory of the gods; and, as we've already discussed, cities like Helike were destroyed when their inhabitants angered the gods.

Science has explained most of these events and phenomena to us, but the stories about these ancient gods still linger and inspire the imagination.

GREECE AND ROME

The Greek gods have proven the most fertile mythology that is still visited today, and rightly so, given the effect of Greek culture on classical Europe. The Greek gods are typically treated as one distinct group, but there are still different local beliefs that change a name or a small relationship. The names and locations are slightly different, but the stories ultimately remain the same. Most of these Greek stories spread to the Roman Empire, with several tales explaining just how and why these gods are at once the same and different.

In all of these Greek and Roman traditions, Apollo is a common figure, a sun god riding his chariot across the sky and looking down on all that he and the other gods had created. Apollo brought warmth and light, and was worshipped as a god of truth and medicine, but there was a small catch to his benevolence: if ever Apollo was wronged or challenged, he would not ride across the sky, plunging the world into eternal darkness.

The Greek gods were also used to describe the seasons, with specific reference to the harvest months – this element of the story is entrenched in adulterous elements that put modern soaps to shame. Hades, god of death and the underworld, wooed Persephone, daughter of Demeter, goddess of the harvest. When Hades kidnapped Persephone and took her to his realm, Demeter was heartbroken and refused to fulfil her duties. To maintain the natural order, Zeus declared that Persephone would spend three months with Hades before returning to Olympus to spend time with the other gods. Those three months coincided with the cold winters, while Persephone's return began the growth of crops in spring.

The story of Persephone bears startling similarities to that of Helen of Troy and the subsequent Trojan War, an episode of Greek military history that occurred around 1200 BC. The Trojan War forms a bridge between many real-world stories and fantastical narratives of the gods, with many using the Trojan War as a starting point for other tales that discuss the gods' interference in the lives of real-life figures. Many of these stories focus on human politics and pride.

In fact, god-like pride was such a sin to the classical Greeks that they had their own word for it: *hubris*. The hubris of several Greek heroes led them to offend the gods and the gods subsequently cursed their families; although this was a recurring theme throughout Greek mythology, the effects of this lesson can still be felt in modern religions and their emphasis on humility.

EGYPT

The Egyptians had an equally complicated relationship with their deities and even used a similar story about gods and their wives to explain a specific geographical cycle.

The River Nile would flood every year, and the Egyptians attributed this to the excessive tears shed by the goddess Isis as she mourned for the apparent death of her husband Osiris; in an incestuous twist that was practised by the Greek gods as well, Osiris was recognised as Isis's brother.

Like many myths and legends, Osiris moved through an ongoing stage of temporary death and rebirth, but this element of eternal life is not limited to the Egyptian deities. Many other gods have mirrored such stories of returning from their own deaths.

THE LEGEND OF THE FIVE SUNS

Although Aztec mythology has its origins several thousand miles away from the Mediterranean, there are many similarities in the interactions between gods. But Aztec mythology goes even further to addressing the End of the World.

Like the Greek and Egyptian stories we've looked at, Aztec mythology pays close attention to cycles, suggesting that there were eras of history ruled over by different gods. We are currently living in the fifth of these eras, with four such ages having already ended and mankind resurrected each time.

During the First Sun, the gods created a race of giants and demigods, but a rivalry arose between the sun god Tezcatlipoca and his rival Quetzalcoatl, who deposed the sun and ordered that the giants be consumed by jaguars.

Quetzalcoatl took control of the Earth during the age of the Second Sun, overseeing the creation of humans, who became less respectful of the gods as the era continued. In anger, Tezcatlipoca turned the people into a race of monkeys who were blown away by hurricanes.

Tlaloc ruled the Third Sun, but after his wife was stolen – by the trouble-making Tezcatlipoca, no less – Tlaloc refused to look after the Earth. He let humanity die in a drought before wiping the Earth clean in a rain of fire.

Chalchiuhtlicue took over for the Fourth Sun, but Tezcatlipoca caused strife between her and humanity, suggesting that she didn't care for her human charges as much as she suggested. A heartbroken Chalchiuhtlicue cried tears of blood, causing a great flood that wiped the Earth clean a fourth time.

Humanity was resurrected one final time under the Fifth Sun of Huitzilopochtli. However, Huitzilopochtli's siblings, the gods of the night, became jealous of his glory, staging nightly attacks on his sun. The Aztec peoples worshiped Huitzilopochtli and prayed for his success in these battles, knowing that if they failed, the world would fall into eternal darkness and end in a great earthquake.

RAGNAROK

The Aztecs were not alone in their specific beliefs about the End of the World: Norse mythology went one step further to develop a complicated theory about the war that would accompany the Endtimes of their own mythology, and exactly how that battle would play out. With so many myths and legends about water and fire, it should come as no surprise that the Norse Apocalypse, or Ragnarok, is a story overflowing with elemental references, whether it's the crashing waves caused by the sea serpent Jormungandr or the flames breathed by the dragon Surtr.

Ragnarok details an epic battle between the Norse gods and their enemies, with humanity caught in the middle. There are also references aplenty to flaming skies, floods and Earth being plunged into darkness. It doesn't take much to draw a line between the image of a flaming sky and the meteors we've already mentioned, nor a darkened Earth as an explanation for an eclipse.

Do we then believe that Ragnarok is a theory about a possible future or, as with these other religions we've discussed, a proto-scientific attempt to explain events as and when they happened?

It's probably the latter: the events of Ragnarok, as outlined in the *Edda* collection of stories and poetry, are strangely specific about the death count amongst the Norse gods, right down to lost limbs, who fights whom and how many steps Thor takes after being poisoned while killing a giant snake.

The comic-book version of Thor that has been appearing in recent movies is a different, fictional take on the same character, but there have been plenty of references and interpretations to Ragnarok and other pieces of Norse myth throughout his lengthy publishing history.

Not only do some of the gods survive Ragnarok, but Norse mythology even has its very own human survivors to repopulate the Earth, Lif and Lifthrasir. Their existence echoes the original role held by the mythological progenitors of humanity, Ask and Embla.

Any similarities to Adam and Eve are just pure coincidence, right?

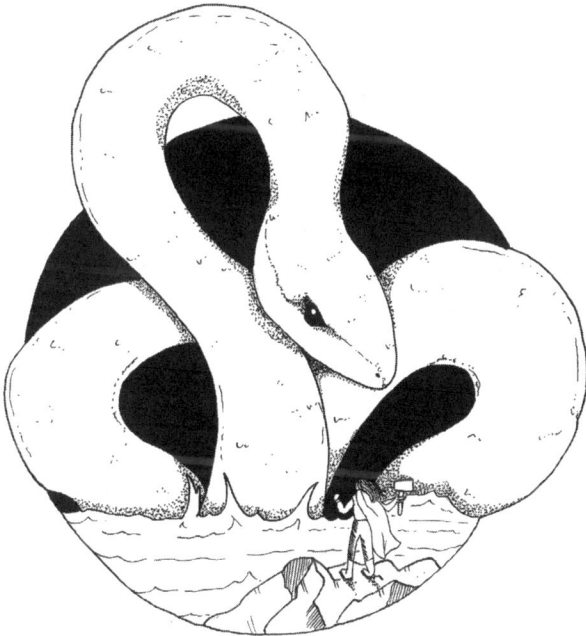

4

THE GOOD BOOK:
ORIGINS OF
THE APOCALYPSE

Despite the intricacies of Ragnarok, Norse mythology is not unique: it is not the only belief system to embrace the Endtimes and is certainly not the only one to have specific stories about how, when and why the End of the World might happen.

Most of the religions we discussed in the previous chapter are no longer practised as major religions: some elements have been adopted as part of New Age worship, with other aspects reduced to inspiration for various works of fiction. Nevertheless, these myths and stories have become so pervasive that words and phrases are used without reference to their origins.

Many of the lessons at the heart of these beliefs can still be seen in modern religions: the most widely practised religions around Europe and the United States are the Abrahamic religions with their common origins, beliefs and literature. Although the similarities between these religions are often underplayed for political purposes, these shared origins to Judaism, Christianity and Islam are made even more obvious with reference to the origins of life and to the End of the World.

Census figures from 2011 indicate that the Abrahamic religions are practised by approximately 65 per cent of the population of the United Kingdom, which is a significant decrease on the figure of 75 per cent in 2001. For both of these surveys, Christianity is the largest single religion recorded, accounting for 59 per cent in 2011 and 70 per cent in 2001.

Befitting such widely practised religions, most of the language and imagery we use to discuss the End of the World in religious terms comes from the beliefs of Judaism, Christianity and Islam. Fire, floods and natural disasters are a primal fear that we all share, regardless of beliefs or location, but these religions specifically tie these into a series of events that will relate to the End of Days.

Although they are known under different names, the books of the Old Testament are common to all three religions and provide the foundations for the modern view of the End of the World. Much of this comes from the first five books of the Old Testament: these are known as the Torah in the Jewish faith and include the books of Genesis, Exodus, Leviticus, Numbers and Deuteronomy. Muslims also venerate these books as part of the divine revelation upon which their religion has been built, although less emphasis is placed on these than on the later parts of the Quran.

The Torah outlines God's creation of the world and its inhabitants, along with the early days of the Jewish peoples.

DIVINE JUDGEMENT

The God of the Old Testament is known for His divine judgements and vengeful ways, and the Abrahamic religions feature as many stories about this as Greek mythology. One of the best-known examples of biblical condemnation comes from the Book of Genesis and involves the cities of Sodom and Gomorrah.

Sodom and Gomorrah were amongst five cities located on the plains beside the River Jordan, just north of the Dead Sea, the other cities were Admah, Zeboim and Bela. The Bible isn't overly explicit about how these cities were corrupted, but Sodom lends its name to the act of sodomy and should give some indication of the stories associated with the area.

After Abraham had visited the area – the same Abraham from whom the religions earn their name – God made clear His intention to destroy the cities. Abraham negotiated with God to save some of the area's more virtuous inhabitants, and his nephew Lot endeavoured to find such people.

Unable to find any virtue within Sodom and Gomorrah, the angels sent to destroy the cities told Lot to flee the area with his family, warning him not to look back at the cities' destruction. As they rained down fire and brimstone, Lot's wife turned back to look at their former home and was turned into a pillar of salt as punishment.

Noah

The concept of the Abrahamic God wiping out whole civilisations is not unique to Sodom and Gomorrah: the Book of Genesis also recounts the story of Noah and the Flood, a story that introduces water in world-ending style in the same way that Sodom and Gomorrah feature fire.

The events of the Flood occur before Sodom and Gomorrah, at a time when God's judgement was directed at the entirety of mankind rather than specific communities. Believing humanity to be corrupt and beyond saving, God planned to flood the Earth, returning it to the primordial state it had been in during the Creation. God made Noah aware of His plans, suggesting that the devout and righteous man should save his family and others that he deemed worthy.

The story of Noah has become well known, especially because of the suggestion that Noah saved two of each animal to help repopulate the Earth. This element in particular has led many different interpretations of whether this episode truly occurred or is meant as a symbolic entry to highlight God's power.

Most modern scholars believe that the story of Noah is more of an attempt to explain natural disasters, reconciling them with the existence of God and suggesting that His good will has led to our continued existence. This interpretation of the story of Noah only serves to highlight the similarities between this and the stories about Ragnarok and the Fourth Sun of Aztec mythology, as well as references to floods throughout other mythologies and epic tales.

Fragments of the Noah story suggest that God's anger might not have been directed at humanity, but rather at a race that was successfully eliminated during the Flood: the Nephilim.

These were born of the unholy union between the sons of God and the daughters of men, but there are different interpretations of what this means: at their most simple, the Nephilim are simply a corrupted rival tribe to Noah's family; at their most fantastic, they are the children of fallen angels taking the form of giants and monsters.

The Book of Daniel

While the books of the Torah provide accounts of the creation and destruction of the Earth, another book in the Old Testament becomes an important feature in discussions about the End of the World, and for good reason.

The Book of Daniel includes dream-like prophecy and revelations as written by the wise man Daniel; this book is treated differently by the Jewish and Christian faiths, with the Christian Bible placing the Book of Daniel alongside books of prophecy, while Judaism treats Daniel as a biography.

The Book of Daniel suggests that, even in hardship, God will save his people: the Babylonian king Nebuchadnezzar has sacked the Temple in Jerusalem and taken Daniel as an advisor, but by adhering to his faith, Daniel is able to provide insight for the king, and ultimately save both his life and the lives of his friends.

Much of the Book of Daniel takes the form of dreams and prophecies that Daniel interprets and provides guidance on: there are references throughout the book to four kingdoms, with a divine fifth kingdom that is yet to come – similar to the five eras of Aztec myth. The book also features beasts and the discussion about future events that resurface throughout the rest of the Bible.

The Book of Daniel is rarely discussed in its own right with regards to the End of the World, but scholars believe it is key to understanding some of the later books of the Bible, especially the Book of Revelations in the New Testament. By combining the two books together, we see a wealth of thought and theories about the Endtimes, and much of Christian eschatology has built on these books.

SIGNS OF THE TIMES

Throughout the Old Testament, there are several references to the ultimate fate of mankind, and these have become the basic foundations of how the modern world looks at the End of the World. Due to the sheer numbers practising the Abrahamic religions, these events and images have become engrained in how we think about the Apocalypse: it's nearly impossible to think about the End of the World without reference to these religions.

The fact that Judaism, Christianity and Islam have such common roots serves to entrench these thoughts about the Endtimes, and a whole wealth of art, culture and political thought has developed around some common themes. In fact, most of these themes can even be found in other religions and beliefs.

The Torah outlines some of the events that are at the heart of the End of the World for the Jewish faith. We'll discuss these elements in a lot more detail over the next few chapters, but you're probably aware of these, regardless of your faith. The Jewish people believe that as part of the End of the World the following will happen:

♦   The Jewish people will be returned to the land of Israel.
♦   A Messiah – specifically from the House of David – will lead the Jewish people.

♦ A new age of global peace will be ushered in, when all will accept and share the Jewish faith.
♦ The dead will be resurrected to share in the new world.

This Jewish vision of the Endtimes gives us some new ways of looking at the End of the World: no longer are we just afraid of the world around us and the whims of angry gods, but we are also given a list of qualities to adhere to, a way of behaving which we should follow in order to avoid meeting our end when the Apocalypse comes.

As the Abrahamic religions each grew in size, thoughts about the End of the World became contentious and exclusive: with multiple faiths and interpretations developing around the same books, there were suddenly different interpretations of the End of the World, with a promise that only some of us would or could be saved, and all the rest would be damned.

5

THE MESSIAH
AND THE
ANTICHRIST

While the notion that a single person can singlehandedly avert the End of the World is laughable, human culture has a fascination with heroic characters, from the gods of classical religions to the superheroes of popular culture in the twentieth century.

As a people, we're ready to embrace heroes and leaders, especially if they can save us from some awful fate – we're also prepared to destroy them if they endanger us.

Heroes aren't confined to religious texts but their role in the End of the World is an important one, whether it's Thor who singlehandedly slays dragons and snakes or Noah who builds the ark on which humanity can escape the flood. The hero doesn't always have to fight battles or lead an army, but he is nonetheless a force to be reckoned with, one who will protect and unite humanity.

This hero is a recurring part of the theories and thoughts about the Apocalypse, and for Judaism, Christianity and Islam, we refer to them as the Messiah. The arrival of the Messiah is an important part of all of these religions, with most religions awaiting his arrival as the culmination of their school of beliefs. With their origins long before a time of gender equality, most of these religions have been dominated by males for centuries, and the Messiah – and God – are usually discussed in masculine terms.

For modern Christians, the Messiah is synonymous with the figure of Jesus Christ, who was born approximately 2,000 years ago and was hailed as the Messiah foreseen by the Jewish faith.

Christianity grew around acceptance of Jesus as the Messiah: his teachings were added to the Old Testament, forming a new religious text that that became the Bible. These new chapters, the New Testament, discuss the life of Jesus and his followers, alongside the early days of the Christian religion; the Gospels of Mark, Matthew, Luke and John were written by Jesus' own followers and specifically record his life, death and resurrection.

Jesus fulfils some of the expectations around the Messiah, but not all of them. He was born to the House of David and there are many passages in the Bible that discuss how he was anointed with oil. The word messiah actually derives from *moshiach*, which literally means 'anointed' and was used to describe any leader who had been anointed with holy oil, whether a priest, king or other wise man.

The details surrounding Jesus' life, as recorded in the Gospels, focus on the fact that Jesus was not seen as the Messiah of the Jewish faith, ultimately leading to his death on the cross and with him rising from the dead three days later. Christians look on this rejection as a struggle that Jesus had to go through, realising that the Messiah would not be accepted by all people until he had experienced trials and tribulations that affirmed his faith.

The Jewish Messiah was also expected to fulfil a number of other tasks, namely with the building of the Third Temple in Jerusalem, the return of all Jews to Israel and the start of an era of world peace that would unite all of humanity; the Jewish rejection of Jesus focuses on these acts, realising that Jesus cannot be the Messiah while these events have not yet occurred.

Jesus' death and resurrection provides much of the imagery used by Christian belief: the cross has become the most obvious representation of Christian faith, a symbol that embodies both love and suffering. However, both the cross and Jesus' death mean nothing without his later resurrection.

In the resurrection, Jesus hints at just one element of the Jewish End of the World that has since become a focal point for the Endtimes: the resurrection of the dead. By a triumphant return from the dead, Jesus proves himself to have mastery over death, a mastery that he promises to share amongst the faithful.

Christians believe that, after his return from the dead, Jesus continued to preach before ultimately rising into Heaven to join God, promising that he would return as part of the End of Days. This should not be treated as another death: Christians believe that Jesus is still alive and that his promised return will, in fact, be seen as him descending from Heaven.

This Second Coming has since been linked to the End of the World and has become an important part of Christian eschatology. As beliefs have grown and developed, different Churches have adopted different attitudes towards the Second Coming: some look forward to it as an event to be celebrated, while others fear its imminent approach. Some even believe that the Second Coming, or *parousia*, has already occurred.

Regardless, Christians believe that the Second Coming is one of the first events to herald the Apocalypse.

JUDAISM

Because the Jewish faith does not recognise Jesus as the Messiah, there are no specific references to the Second Coming as a sign of the Endtimes: once the Messiah appears it will, in fact, be the first coming. However, by claiming to be the Messiah, Jesus Christ fulfilled a different role, that of a false messiah who both led humanity astray and tested the faith and conviction of the faithful.

There are, however, some commenters and philosophers who try to reconcile Judaism and Christianity by suggesting that after his Second Coming, Jesus Christ will fulfil the various prophecies and roles of the Messiah, proving himself to have been the Jewish Messiah all along.

CHRISTIANITY

With the Second Coming forming such an important part of the Christian faith, it should come as no surprise that there have been many different theories about how, when and why this will happen.

The Second Coming has taken a number of forms over the last 2,000 years and has commonly reflected the political climates of any given time. Some believe that Jesus will be born again in conditions that echo his first birth; others believe that the Second Coming will be a dramatic affair with loud noises and lights in the sky.

There are also different suggestions as to what role Jesus will play during this Second Coming, and again, most of these depend on the politics of the time and the location of the Church. During his original time on Earth, Jesus was hailed as a wise man and teacher, but Jesus may return as a warrior, ready to fight the battles that will accompany the End of Days.

Even the depictions of Jesus as a warrior differ, with some Churches suggesting that Jesus will use divine powers and abilities to show his power and might to overcome adversity, while others imply that Jesus will don a suit of armour and lead the charge at the head of a Christian army.

All of these interpretations agree that Jesus' Second Coming will be at a time to save humanity from a great threat, whether that threat is created by mankind itself, or whether it comes from an external source. After all, if Jesus is to lead mankind in a battle, he needs a force to fight against.

ISLAM

The Islamic faith has been subject to a lot of misinformation: the origins that it shares with Judaism and Christianity are often forgotten in favour of politics and scaremongering, turning Islam into a terrifying alternative that opposes Christianity. It's a situation that has led to wars and acts of violence around the world for hundreds of years, violence that is still seen today.

In reality, Islam has close ties to Christianity and Judaism, with many locations and prayers important to all three faiths. The Islamic holy book, the Quran, builds upon the teachings of the Jewish and Christian faiths, adding the teachings of Muhammad as written in the sixth century. Saints and prophets are common to all three faiths: although Jesus is not at the heart of Islam, as in Christianity, he continues to be a key figure with an important role to play in both the religion and the salvation of mankind.

Muslims do not believe that Jesus is the Son of God, but they do believe he was the Messiah and was sent to teach humanity how to better follow God's teachings. The circumstances of Jesus' life remain the same as in the Christian Bible. However, certain Muslims do not believe that Jesus was crucified at the end of his life but rather that one of Jesus' disciples posed as him in order to save Jesus.

For Muslims, Jesus fulfils the role of a prophet, sent to prepare the world for the coming of the 'Mahdi', the redeemer and saviour: when Mahdi arrives, it is Jesus who will call attention to him and acknowledge him as the saviour. As such, Jesus fulfils a role roughly equivalent to John the Baptist in the Christian faith.

Most of the Muslim beliefs about Jesus (or 'Isa') portray Jesus as the right hand of Mahdi and therefore instrumental in the events of the Endtimes.

Mahdi himself is not explicitly mentioned in the Quran, but is revered throughout the Muslim tradition. Like the Messiah, there are different beliefs as to how and when Mahdi will appear, whether he will be born of humanity like Jesus, or if he will descend from Heaven alongside Jesus' Second Coming.

THE FORCES OF EVIL

Just as the classical religions and mythologies pitted gods against each other, giving enemies to our heroes and saviours, the Abrahamic religions have done the same thing.

In fact, most of these enemies are descended from the gods of ancient religions, being the embodiments of some natural event that mankind doesn't fully comprehend. In other cases, this evil is the embodiment of some sin, attempting to corrupt humanity.

With these enemies in mind, the idea of an Antichrist was born, a figure that will stand against the Messiah and saviour. Different religions have different interpretations of the Antichrist, from a sinister evil to a simple nuisance, but he is a common figure throughout Judaism, Christianity and Islam.

Christians, Jews and Muslims believe that all things were created by God, who continues to have power over all things: evil becomes a complicated concept, something that was once affiliated with God but is now a force or an individual that works against God's will.

Like the Messiah, the different versions of the Antichrist have been coloured by politics and location. In some cases, the Antichrist is a false Messiah who will corrupt humanity and lead them astray, taking a back seat in the final events of the Apocalypse; others describe him as a Man of Sin with unnatural powers who will be brought into direct conflict with the Messiah.

This vision of the Antichrist is unique to the religions we have been discussing: typically, evil beings in other religions were simply a misunderstood god of mischief, a monster or beast, or a force or energy that runs through all things. This form of the Antichrist is, instead, a physical entity that is as connected to humanity as the Messiah himself: he is a figure to be both feared and revered, whether his role is an active one or one of more subtle corruption.

Most visions of the End of the World incorporate the Antichrist or a similar evil force: if the Messiah is to arrive in order to save humanity from evil, it makes some sense that this evil might be the Antichrist. As some Churches look for signs of the Second Coming as the trigger for the Endtimes, others suggest that the Antichrist will arrive first, becoming the reason for the Messiah's necessary return.

The Abrahamic religions have a host of enemy-like figures to stand alongside the Antichrist in opposition to God, with the Bible openly acknowledging demons as enemies of Heaven. Through miracles, Jesus and the saints have faced these demons, casting them out of human bodies.

There are some encounters within the Bible which suggest that these demons exist in great numbers and cannot be simply overcome by prayer alone. During one such exorcism conducted by Jesus among the Gerasenes, a demon confronts Jesus directly, suggesting that its name is 'Legion', because it is one of many.

Various writers have attempted to examine the Bible and other religious texts in order to discover more about these demons – the results have been terrifying.

Johann Weyer, Alphonso de Spina and Gregory of Nyssa have all suggested that there are actually millions of demons, operating in a complex hierarchy that involves dukes and generals. These same writers suggest that some of these demons were once agents of God, fallen angels who were cast out after rebelling against Him.

The leader of these fallen angels has given us a name that has become synonymous with the Antichrist, while suggesting some much darker evil: Satan.

Satan and Lucifer

Lucifer and Satan are words used throughout the Bible to refer to the same person, the most active of the fallen angels and the one who has since become associated with the figure of the Antichrist. The Devil is treated as the chief of the demons of Hell, and therefore a force of evil that will rival God. Typically, these are discussed in the same breath, with the fallen angel of Satan having taken on the identity of the Devil after falling from God's favour.

There are many different stories about the fall of these angels. Fictional accounts such as John Milton's epic poem *Paradise Lost* paint Lucifer as a proud character who has much in common with the tragic heroes of Shakespearean and Greek tragedy. However, within the Bible, Satan's villainy is a lot more obvious, and he is an active corrupting force of humanity in both the Old and New Testaments.

In the Old Testament, Satan appears in the Garden of Eden, taking the form of a snake to urge Adam and Eve towards sin. The duo challenge God's authority by eating the fruit of a forbidden tree and are cast out of Eden, condemning their descendants, humanity itself, to forever be haunted by Original Sin.

Satan also appears to Jesus directly in the Gospel, tempting him during the forty days and nights of solitude that he spends in the desert. As Jesus prepares to accept his fate as the Son of God and preach, Satan's manipulations are more subtle as he encourages Jesus to use his divine nature to escape his self-imposed fast.

While Satan is often mentioned in the same breath as the Antichrist, there are many interpretations of the Bible that make sure to treat both of these individuals separately; in fact, the Book of Revelations, the main source for Christian thoughts on the End of the World, mentions multiple distinct beasts and enemies during the End of Days. There is little doubt that Satan and the Antichrist will be in league, but attributing their evil to one figure alone implies that they will be individually more powerful than the Bible suggests.

In some places, Satan is called Lucifer, although this adds some complications to the concept of Satan as an 'evil' figure as the name Lucifer has not always been treated as an evil name in Christian thought.

Lucifer of Cagliari was a fourth-century bishop in Sardinia, Italy, and even though the Church does not recognise him as a saint, the locals nonetheless refer to him as Saint Lucifer.

Lucifer is also called the Morning Star, or Lightbringer, a figure associated with the planet Venus and the sun itself. The stories of the fallen angels, with Lucifer at their head, could actually be a reference to the worship of false gods, with the God of the Abrahamic religions displacing the sun gods of pagan mythology. This interpretation acknowledges some importance for these gods: rather than dismissing them completely, they become fallen angels who were doomed to fall through their own pride, only to be replaced by God directly.

The Antichrist in Judaism

Because the Jewish Messiah is yet to arrive, Judaism does not recognise an Antichrist as a rival to Jesus. Instead, the Antichrist is any one of the many false prophets, or *pseudochristos*, who will distract humanity and lead them astray from the path of the true Messiah. It is possible that the word 'Antichrist' has been created by an error in translating this word, adopting some of the other negative elements in the process.

In Jewish belief, Jesus would actually fulfil the role of a *pseudochristos*, or Antichrist, in that he is seen as a false Messiah.

There are still references throughout Jewish texts from the Middle Ages to an evil figure, a king and leader called Armilius who would be born of the union between Satan and a virgin. Armilius would rise to become a king, coming into conflict with the Jewish Messiah. Since Armilius is missing from the Bible and other canonical texts, he is not accepted as a legitimate Antichrist figure and may even have been used as a metaphor for Jesus in antichristian propaganda.

The Antichrist in Islam

Contrary to Judaism, the Antichrist plays a very specific role in the Endtimes of Islamic beliefs, although his origins are closer to the Jewish *pseudochristos* than Satan or the Devil.

The Muslim Antichrist is named Al-Masih ad-Dajjall, literally meaning 'false prophet' or 'deceiver', and he is the last in a line of thirty such deceivers. He has no right eye, and his left eye sparkles like a star.

The coming of the Dajjall coincides with a period of decadence amongst society when governments become corrupt and prayers are no longer spoken. The Dajjall becomes the leader of these corrupt forces until he comes up against Jesus and Mahdi. In fact, in some schools of Muslim belief, it is Jesus, not Mahdi, who is ultimately victorious over Dajjall.

6

THE BOOK OF
REVELATIONS

With all the similarities between the Abrahamic religions, there is little truly unique to the Christian Apocalypse; however, the size and breadth of the numbers practising Christianity has meant that this Christian flavour to the End of the World has become the most pervasive and lasting. This vision has also become the easiest to adopt and manipulate by other sources, creating no end of movies, books and other media that attempt to portray the End of the World.

This uniquely Christian version of the Endtimes mostly comes from the Book of Revelations, the last book of the New Testament. This is the book that lends us the word apocalypse, linking the word forever with the world-ending events that the book describes.

Although the Book of Revelations provides a near-complete resource in Christian eschatology, the imagery found within is actually collected from other sources: some elements of Revelations make it a sequel to the Old Testament's Book of Daniel, with this book expanding on some references and adding much more detail.

The Book of Revelations takes the form of a dream and a possible series of events that lead to the End of Days. However, because the book highlights its own nature, calling attention to the dream within it, it has led to many different interpretations, with different Churches and beliefs responding to the book in different ways.

With all these different interpretations, little about the Book of Revelations can be taken at face value and trusted, although there are still people who read the book as a literal guide to how the End of the World will come about. The imagery and events described in the book have taken on a life of their own, discussed outside of a religious context and taking on meanings to people who would not identify themselves as Christian.

The writer of the Book of Revelations identifies himself as John, with some theologians thinking that this is the evangelist of the same name, one of Jesus' Twelve Apostles and writer of the Gospel of John. However, John was a common name during this time, with many taking the name in honour of either the Apostle or John the Baptist.

John's dream describes the many tribulations that will come in the End of Days, outlining what will happen to both those who remain faithful to God and those who rise up as enemies. Revelations also collects some of the Bible's most explicit references to an enemy of God, discussing several beasts that are linked to Satan, the Devil and the Antichrist:

♦ A dragon with seven heads who throws the stars to the Earth, and is revealed to be Satan.
♦ A seven-headed leopard – that the dragon gives power to – emerges from the sea and blasphemes against God.
♦ A beast with seven heads and ten horns, which emerges from the Earth and is known by its number, 666.

THE BEAST OF THE EARTH

The three beasts of revelations are often discussed as one: even though they are treated as different creatures, they are all connected in their origin and are usually seen as a metaphor for the forces of the Earth, namely the air, sea and earth, turning against humanity.

These enemies grow all the more powerful during the Endtimes, gaining followers across the globe, and their actions bring the full extent of God's vengeance upon the Earth in a series of natural disasters:

♦ The sea and waters of the Earth turn to blood.
♦ The sun burns the Earth and then the Earth falls into darkness.
♦ A great earthquake levels the Earth.

The climax to these disasters leads to the End of the World that we have already discussed; all nations embrace and begin to follow God and those who are not faithful are struck down, with the various beasts and enemies cast into the lake of fire. Satan is imprisoned for 1,000 years, during which Jesus rules the Earth. After this time, Satan rises once more to wage war against Heaven but is finally defeated and destroyed. Finally, Heaven and Earth are reborn and the dead are resurrected.

Muslim belief also references a different beast of the Earth, a being called Dabbat al-Ard. This beast is a symbol of the coming Endtimes, but where the Christian beasts of Revelations are seen as destructive forces, Dabbat al-Ard is sent by God to remind humanity of His presence and His power. Since the Muslim Apocalypse coincides with a massive loss of faith, the beast arrives as a sort of last warning to remind people of the faith they have now lost.

Even acknowledging the metaphors and dream-like qualities, Revelations is a complicated text, and one that theologians and scholars have spent nearly 2,000 years trying to interpret, unsure how deeply to read into the codes and hidden meanings of the book. Some of the imagery might appear obvious from the various destructive acts and elements to the key players and locations in the book.

However, there have been so many readings of Revelations that persons of faith could find hints about the End of the World wherever they might look.

THE NUMBER OF THE BEAST

Immortalised by *The Omen* and an Iron Maiden song, a wealth of superstition surrounds the number 666. In fact, the fear of this seemingly arbitrary, if somewhat repetitive, number even has its own lengthy name: hexakosioihexekontahexaphobia.

While this number itself has a peculiar relation to the Book of Revelations, a fear of numbers is common in other cultures as well: many readers are probably untrusting of the number 13, while Japanese and Chinese culture associate the same superstitions with the number 4 due to its similarities to the word for 'hell'.

Like much of the Book of Revelations, the number of the Beast is open to many interpretations, with some sources stating that the number is actually 616, with translation problems leading to the 666 that we currently know. Some of the demonologists we've already discussed linked this number to demons and the forces of Hell, suggesting that each of the 666 legions of Hell contains 666 demons.

However, this number may not be a number at all, but rather a name: the Hebrew alphabet uses numbers and letters interchangeably, usually relying on context to indicate which is used.

So what does the number 666 spell?

It's not an exact art, but there are two possible names that come up when applying this method: the king Nebuchadnezzar who captured Jerusalem in the seventh century BC and is featured in the Book of Daniel; and Neron Cessar, or Nero, ruler of the Roman Empire in the middle of the first century AD, at a time roughly contemporary to the writing of the Book of Revelations.

Written in Roman numerals, 666 is DCLXVI (500 + 100 + 50 + 10 + 5 + 1) and features one occurrence of every roman numeral under 1,000 (M), all in descending order.

Also, 666 is an important number in science, although in a form unlikely to have been known at the time of Revelations. Carbon-12, which is found in all living beings, has six protons, six electrons and six neutrons.

GOG AND MAGOG

Gog and Magog are mentioned throughout the Bible but are key players in the Book of Revelations, the names of a destructive force that will be marshalled by Satan at the End of Days. They will be followers of the beasts, enemies of Heaven, and will persecute those that follow Jesus.

It's unclear whether Gog and Magog are individuals, tribes or geographic locations: throughout the Bible, names of well-known individuals are adopted by their families and the areas in which they live. The earliest biblical reference to Magog is in the Book of Genesis where Magog is the grandson of Noah. A later reference is to Gog from the land of Magog, which implies that Gog may be descended from the earlier Magog.

The Book of Revelations pairs Gog and Magog together, treating them as a pair who combine their efforts to thwart mankind and the Messiah.

If Gog and Magog are a location, they have no fixed or definite place: as with much of the Bible, many locations have long since changed names, with some cities and cultures falling into obscurity.

However, certain translations of the Bible add further meanings to these words. For example, a Greek version of the Old Testament uses Gog in place of Agag when discussing a classical king who fought against Saul, the first King of Israel. If Gog is to be considered a historical figure, then Revelations may actually hint at the past rather than the future. Agag is also translated as 'flame', which only adds another level of meaning to the destruction that Gog brings, as Gog may not be person or army but simply a destructive fire.

The Islamic interpretation of Revelations specifies that Gog and Magog are nations, with the similarly named Ya'jooj and Ma'jooj. In the Islamic Apocalypse, these nations are located in a place where east meets west.

On a journey through this area, the righteous ruler Dhul-Qarnayn – often identified as Alexander the Great – is asked to build a wall to protect the virtuous tribes of the area from the warlike Ya'jooj and Ma'jooj. Dhul-Qarnayn helps to build the wall, but suggests to the natives that, at the End of Days, God will reduce the wall to dust and these tribes will spread across the Earth, wreaking destruction once more.

THE FOUR HORSEMEN
AND THE SEVEN SEALS

As the Book of Revelations progresses, it reveals a scroll or book held in God's right hand – the same side on which Jesus apparently sits. Seven seals keep this scroll closed, but as the beasts and Gog and Magog make their presence known, moving across the Earth, God breaks each seal and opens the scroll.

With the breaking of each seal, the End of the World edges ever closer, with the first four seals summoning forth the most enduring images of the Apocalypse: the Four Horsemen.

These horsemen arrive accompanied by an otherworldly voice saying, 'Come and see'. They then ride across the Earth, marshalling the faithful to God's side and striking down their enemies. However, the horsemen also act as a stark reminder of God's wrath if people were to turn against their faith. Each of the riders is identified by a differently coloured horse and a weapon or totem, with only the fourth horseman named.

♦   The first horseman is depicted on a white horse, wearing a crown on his head and carrying a bow and arrows. This rider is given many names, but is typically recognised as Conquest.

♦   The second horseman rides a red horse and is given a large sword and the power to make men kill each other. With his sword and affinity to death and the act of killing, this horseman is recognised as War.

♦   The third horseman rides a black horse, and is the only one of the Four Horsemen to speak. He carries a balancing scales, talking about the price of wheat, oil and wine: he is recognised as Famine.

♦   The final horseman is the only one of the four to be named in the Book of Revelations, and rides a pale horse. He is called Death, and he is followed closely by Hell. Different interpretations imply that Death is an evil figure and commands the demonic armies of Hell; others suggest that this reference to Hell is the combined mass of every person who has ever died, with Death restoring them to their place in the new world. There is also a suggestion that Death has enslaved the old pagan gods of death. Like Jesus, he is a master of death itself, making this pale rider a powerful figure.

Although the Four Horsemen are not destructive figures, their affinity to the End of the World has led to them becoming feared characters and harbingers of death and destruction. Some works of art separate them entirely from their biblical origins, focusing only on their role as bringers of doom. To further build the fear of these figures, the White Rider is often transformed from Conquest into Pestilence or Plague.

Of course, this reading neglects the fact that the Four Horsemen are summoned by, and presumably answerable to, God.

With an emphasis on the Four Horsemen, the Seven Seals are often neglected, especially the fifth, sixth and seventh of their number. The final seals are actually closer to an Apocalypse that we have already discussed, bringing home the existing ideas about the End of the World. The fifth seal resurrects martyrs and anyone who has died for their faith, winning their assistance in the final battle; the sixth seal signals a great earthquake and a rain of stars; and the seventh seal ushers in a moment of darkness and silence.

ARMAGEDDON

After Revelations introduces the key players in the End of the World, the stage is set for them to clash in a final battle. That battle takes the form of another by-word for the Endtimes: Armageddon.

The literal meaning of Armageddon refers to the site of the final battle involving these key players, with Jesus, the saints and the faithful battle on the side of God while the Antichrist, Satan and the beasts provide the enemies. There are no interpretations as to how long this battle will last, but it will lead to the defeat of the Antichrist and the beasts, with Satan cast into the pit for a period of 1,000 years as punishment for his deeds. However, Satan is not killed or defeated: this final victory is reserved for a time when Satan returns.

Armageddon may actually be a real place, as the name bears close similarities to Tel Megiddo, an ancient settlement about 150km north of Jerusalem.

GEHENNA

After Satan has been cast into the pit, he will return for one final battle; it is only then, with the ultimate defeat of Satan, that Heaven and Earth can be reborn and that all of the dead will rise again. Satan is ultimately defeated when Jesus casts him and his followers into a lake of fire.

Just as Armageddon provides the location of a climactic battle, this final battle is tied to a specific place, with all the clues pointing towards the valley of Gehenna, just outside Jerusalem. The valley was used as both a burial grounds and a site for pagan sacrifices, making if especially fitting as the final resting place of a fallen angel. Gehenna was so closely linked to the concept of death that it has become a Jewish by-word for Hell and the afterlife.

Gehenna is also acknowledged as a place of fire, as many of the sacrifices that took place there involved fire and flames.

Since Gehenna is not an actual lake of fire, this reading suggests that Revelations was not written to be read around the world, but rather has some specific meanings to those familiar with the history and geography of the Israel of the time.

7

READING REVELATIONS: INTERPRETATIONS AND HIDDEN MEANINGS

As we've already seen, there are many different interpretations of the Book of Revelations: some offer a terrifying vision of the End of the World and the fantastical events that will usher in this period; others are far more subtle, a reference to established books and history with political promises and threats about what will befall the enemies of the faithful.

In this chapter, we'll look at just some of the meanings that can be read into Revelations, using codes and references that take into account the time and place in which the book was written.

Revelations may not have been written as one complete text, with the book gathered from a variety of different sources. The earliest fragments of the book date from AD 70, meaning that Revelations was written during the first Jewish-Roman war. Also known as the Great Revolt, this was an attempted rebellion by the Jewish peoples against the Roman Empire that had been occupying Israel for over 100 years. The war came to a bloody climax in the Siege of Jerusalem, where parts of the city were burned and Roman forces destroyed the Temple.

A Preterist reading of Revelations adopts this as its starting point, looking at all of the imagery discussed within the book as a reference to contemporary events: the word has its origins in the Latin word *praetor* meaning past, implying that the contents of Revelations are firmly historical.

SEVEN

The number seven occurs multiple times throughout the Book of Revelations: there are Seven Seals and many different beasts with seven heads.

Seven is also a number used in reference to Rome, the city built on seven hills, with the city itself – and its associated empire – becoming a sort of beast with seven heads.

The Whore of Babylon, referenced in Revelations, is also a false idol who – like Rome – stands atop seven mountains.

Between the death of Jesus in AD 33 and the Siege of Jerusalem in AD 70, there are seven Roman emperors, each the head of an enemy to the Jewish and Christian peoples.

NERO

We have already seen that Nero's name may feature directly in Revelations as the number of the Beast, and there are several aspects of his life and rule that make his inclusion fitting.

Nero was the Roman emperor for fourteen years from AD 54, one of the longest serving emperors of this early Christian period. He was also one of the most active in the persecution of Christians, killing and torturing Christians throughout the Roman Empire.

Even in the present day, Nero's name is become synonymous with corrupt government and rulers. He is known for his pride and extravagant taste: he portrayed himself as an idol to the Roman Empire, in a role that many Christians would have considered blasphemous.

The historian Tacitus noted that Nero had a specific loathing of Christians that went far beyond civic duty and protection of the Empire: Christian slaves and prisoners were tied up in his personal gardens, doused in oil and then burned at the stake in order to provide nightly illumination for his estate and the rest of the city.

This is not the only story that links Nero to fire and destruction: the Great Fire of Rome occurred in AD 64 and destroyed most of the city. Many of the destroyed buildings were in the area of Nero's palaces, with some of them sitting on land marked for future extensions. Some people suggested that Nero ordered these fires himself to make way for his own building work and extending his own wealth.

FOUR

The horsemen introduces the number four to Revelations: these characters may be a reference to the four Roman emperors following Nero, all of whom held power for only a short period of time.

Nero took his own life in AD 68 following revolts and unrest throughout the Empire. His death created a power vacuum and led to the Year of Four Emperors, when Galba, Otho, Vitellius and Vespasian came to rule in quick succession. Galba, Otho and Vitellius all faced opposition, dying quickly, with only Vespasian bringing an end to the period of uncertainty with his lengthy reign.

Each of these four emperors possessed traits that are similar to those of the Four Horsemen:

♦ Galba was a stern ruler who used force to keep tight control over the coffers and taxes of the Empire.

♦ Otho bought his way into power, using his private soldiers to attain the role of Emperor.

♦ Vitelius can be compared to the famine-like third horseman: he is described as a glutton who would order extravagant feasts four times a day, often at the houses of the other nobles.

♦ Finally, Vespasian ruled for ten years and was a key player in the Jewish Revolt and the Siege of Jerusalem. Although Vespasian's attitude towards the Jewish people has been recorded as being quite favourable, the high death toll during this period means that it isn't a stretch to believe that he could have been associated with Death.

THE MILLENNIUM

Prior to his final battle with Jesus, Satan is sentenced to 1,000 years in the pit and, as such, the number has become an important part of the Apocalypse. This millennium has become increasingly more important in modern times, with the passing of any period of 1,000 years becoming a landmark to be acknowledged.

Few of the dates in the Bible should be taken at face value, especially within Revelations: it's possible that these thousand years are an exaggeration of the hundred years that the Roman Empire had been ruling over Israel at the time of writing.

The millennium has since become an important part of philosophy and religion, lending its name to other fields that are not associated with religion or with Revelations. Millenarianism is a general acknowledgement of a great change that will come to the world and may refer to technological or cultural advancement, or perhaps some discovery that will improve quality of life.

Millennialism acknowledges this 1,000 years in which Satan is banished to the pit, and looks forward with hope to the period when this occurs, seeing it as a golden age for humanity when Jesus' reign over the Earth is unaffected by greed or other evils.

There are other beliefs that further expand on millennialism, each belonging to different Churches and speaking volumes about their opinions on the End of the World: premillennialism is the belief that Jesus' Second Coming will take place before the 1,000-year peace, and his reign will be literal and physically on this Earth; postmillennialism is the belief that the 1,000 years will occur before Jesus' Second Coming and that the events of Armageddon will take place in Heaven, not on Earth; and amillennialism completely rejects the importance of the number 1,000 and views this millennium, and the rest of the Book of Revelations, as nothing more than a symbol.

8

THE END OF
THE WORLD IN
OTHER RELIGIONS

Judaism, Islam and Christianity may be the most widely practised religions in the United Kingdom and Europe, but they do not have exclusive rights to the End of the World. In fact, the similarities that we have seen between the Abrahamic religions and some of our more primal fears extend to other religions as well.

ZOROASTRIANISM

Zoroastrianism is not a widely practised modern religion, but it has had a significant impact on modern philosophy and it is also one of the clearest religious examples of the struggle between good and evil.

Zoroastrianism has its origins in Ancient Persia – modern Iran – where the philosopher Zoroaster, or Zarathustra, collected various local beliefs to form one unified religion for the area. Zoroaster recognised a dual nature for humanity, realising that both mankind and nature itself are torn between good and evil, between order and chaos, or, to use the Zoroastrian names, between Ahura Mazda and Angra Mainyu, or Ahriman.

Ahura Mazda, no relation to the motoring brand, is a creative force, with the literal translation meaning 'light of wisdom'; its opposing force, Ahriman, leans towards darkness and destruction. One of the defining aspects of Zoroastrianism is that both of these

forces are equally powerful and exist independently of the other: both energies complement each other, with difficulty arising when they are no longer in balance. This is an interesting comparison to the Christian view of good and evil where Satan as the Devil is depicted as a fallen angel and, as such, created by God.

Zoroastrian beliefs also place special emphasis on the divinity and purity of water and fire, both of which are considered necessary for life.

The Endtimes of the Zoroastrian faith, or *frashokereti*, depicts a final triumph of good energy over evil after a battle between the agents of good – *yazata* – and the *daevas*, or forces of evil. A Messianic figure, Saoshyant, will play a pivotal role in this battle, after which he will resurrect the dead. All of humanity will be judged by passing through a molten river, which will not harm the good, but will burn away those who are evil. Those who are deemed righteous will be granted immortality and will live amongst the *yazatas* in a state close to godliness.

This complicated vision of the End of the World predates Christianity and Revelations by several hundred years: Zoroaster lived around the sixth century BC but the religion is based on local beliefs that go back much further.

BAHÁ'I

The Bahá'i faith is often treated as one of the Abrahamic religions – it has shared origins with Judaism, Christianity and Islam – but the practise of the religion places a great emphasis on faith itself and any display of faith, regardless of the Church or individual beliefs. As such, the religion does not see itself as different from other religions, but rather that all religions share their faith, with all practising different elements of the same beliefs.

The Bahá'i faith sees the central figures of all religions as messengers from God to provide for the needs of his people at any given time. Religious truth comes not in one moment or one teaching, but through 'progressive revelations' that furthers the development and evolution of religion and humanity. There is no true Endtime in Bahá'i, but a period that brings an end to the belief system of one culture or religion and then opens up another.

Bahá'i has its origins in the mid-nineteenth century when the spiritual leader, the Báb, claimed to be the coming of the Muslim Messiah, or Mahdi. The Báb also wrote that he would be followed by another figure, 'He whom God shall make manifest', the final messiah figure that is common to many Eastern and Western religions and philosophies.

The Báb was executed for heresy, but one of his followers, Bahá'u'lláh continued his teachings and later claimed to be the predicted 'He whom God shall make manifest'. Bahá'u'lláh's goal was to unite humanity under one religion and one cause that would acknowledge and respect all of the beliefs that had gone before. As such, the Bahá'i faith believes that Bahá'u'lláh's existence brings an end to the process of progressive revelation, and that the next stage of enlightenment will not be achieved until humanity accepts his teachings.

During his life, Bahá'u'lláh wrote a book called *The Seven Valleys*, which outlined the various levels of enlightenment that the human spirit must travel through. These are Search, Love, Knowledge, Unity, Contentment, Wonderment, True Poverty and

Absolute Nothingness. Absolute Nothingness might sound like an act of ultimate destruction, similar to that found in the Endtimes, but this stage actually involves closeness to God, during which the spirit is reduced to nothing in the glory of God's presence.

TAOISM

Taoism is more of a system and practice for belief than an organised religion. The word *tao* is translated as 'way' and the faith emphasises the practices for a way of life that respects the natural order in all things, without necessarily attributing that to the worship of a god.

There are, however, still gods in the Taoist belief, and like many of the other beliefs we've discussed, there is a prophesied Endtime which will occur at a time when worship and virtue fall into decline.

Taoism also has its own Messianic figure in Li Hong, a potential reincarnation or descendant of Laozi, the writer of the Tao Te Ching, Taoism's holy book. Li Hong is foretold to arrive to settle a great disturbance in the order of Heaven and Earth; like many messianic characters, Li Hong would also rescue a chosen people who would be marked by their devotion, virtues and practices during their life.

BUDDHISM

Buddhism is based around the teachings of the Buddha, or 'the enlightened one', a teacher in Northern India around the sixth century BC. Buddha's teachings aim to help humanity to set aside their suffering and achieve enlightenment and contentment. This is not a short journey, and the concept of rebirth is integral to Buddhist belief, and the spiritual journey continues well after the individual's physical death.

Buddhists do not believe in a God so much as in the cosmic force of Karma, a force that drives our ongoing rebirth, with good

deeds and thoughts rewarded in later stages of the spiritual journey. Buddha foresaw the decline of both his teachings and the Buddhist faith after 5,000 years when society would collapse and require the coming of a new spiritual figure, Maitreya, who would make himself known when the teachings of the Buddha had been completely forgotten, meaning that humanity most needs spiritual salvation.

The number seven also occurs in Buddhist eschatology: in the 'Sermon of the Seven Suns', Buddha outlines a possible End of the World scenario where the appearance of a second sun – and five subsequent suns – will dry the Earth and turn everything to sand and dust until it meets a final fiery end.

Rather than a prediction about the End of the World, the Sermon of the Seven Suns can be read as a meditation on the cyclical nature of Buddhism, and a gentle reminder that even the ongoing cycle of karma and rebirth is not infinite. Like many other cultures and religions, the Buddhist world may still end in destructive fire, and if you have not lived an appropriate life prior to the end, you will not be saved.

Buddhist teachings have been adopted around the world, and even spread to other religions as a means to meditation and spiritual happiness, with the languages of karma passing into secular use.

HINDUISM

Hinduism is the world's third largest religion and is probably one of the world's oldest traditions. But referring to Hinduism as a religion is a problem in itself: this faith is practised across Asia, with many individuals incorporating elements of local beliefs, folklore and even other religions into their practices, including Buddhist meditation and karma. Other aspects of Hinduism embrace a polytheistic approach, similar to the classical religions with their families of warring gods.

With the scope and breadth of the practices it incorporates, Hinduism has no central authority, nor a canon or scripture to adhere to. There are so many differences in the Hindu belief system that it is even possible to reconcile atheism with Hinduism by using the Hindu practices to meditate and ponder on the self and creation, rather than a god in any form.

One facet of Hinduism suggests that there is a single divine being with three different roles: Brahma, the creator; Vishnu, the overseer; and Shiva, the destroyer. All three are responsible for moving the world through a continuous cycle of creation, life, destruction and rebirth.

There are four stages, or *Yugas*, to this cycle, each corresponding with a decline in virtue. Over the course of these four yugas, Vishnu the overseer takes on different roles according to the needs of the world. At the end of each cycle, Vishnu becomes Shiva in order to destroy the world and is then transformed into Brahma in order to remake it.

The final yuga, the era closest to destruction, is called the Kali Yuga, or the 'age of vice'. The name Kali is taken to refer to a demon of sin, but it is also the name of the separate goddess who is the consort of Shiva. During the Kali Yuga, the demon Kali will come into conflict with the final avatar of Vishnu; humanity will find itself lost in drink and drugs, rulers will become corrupt and unjust, and worship of the gods will fade.

In Hindu thought, an avatar is a manifestation or incarnation of a god, which covers both their descent or appearance to interact with humanity on an earthly plane and also the notion that they could be reborn in human form.

The Kali Yuga brings an avatar of Vishnu to Earth, fulfilling a role known as Kalki, as he rides on a white horse, armed with a blazing sword – the similarities to the Four Horsemen should not be ignored.

Kalki and Kali will engage in a great battle between good and evil, with Kali assisted by his twin generals Koka and Vikoka, demons that bear similarities in both names and actions to the biblical Gog and Magog.

Once evil has been defeated, Kalki will rule the Earth for a period of 1,000 years in a new golden age, that will restart the cycle of four yugas.

9

THE HOME OF THE APOCALYPSE: POLITICS OF THE MIDDLE EAST

Most of the religions and beliefs we have looked at so far have their origins in in the Mediterranean and Middle East. With so many faiths blossoming in the region, it should come as no surprise that politics have gotten involved.

Many of the locations that are holy or sacred to one faith are shared by others, and the possession of these landmarks has become a bone of contention. Some of these issues have focused on the potential dangers of the End of the World, others have threatened to bring that moment ever closer.

THE CRUSADES

One of the bloodiest periods of human history, the Crusades, began in the eleventh century AD and were a series of incursions into the Middle East from Europe. There are many reasons behind the Crusades, some political, some religious and some motivated entirely by wealth. By the time of the Crusades, most of central Europe was united under the Holy Roman Empire, a sort of precursor to the European Union. As the name suggests, the Holy Roman Empire was defined by its shared religion, and this religion affected how it reacted with other nations, leading to increased hostility with the neighbouring – and mostly Muslim – Byzantine Empire.

The Crusades arose from a European need to see Jerusalem freed from the oppression and ownership of the Byzantine Empire, assuring access for Christian pilgrims. The Crusades may also have been, simply, an ideological war between Christianity and the growing faith of Islam.

The Crusades lasted for nearly 200 years, with different countries leading the charge under different leaders and regimes: it's safe to say that over that period, motivations shifted significantly, with different causes coming to the fore at any given time.

There were nine Crusades undertaken by the Holy Roman Empire between 1095 and 1272, but not all of these involved every major state. There were also several other incursions undertaken by individual countries or noblemen, with even more were organised by faithful laypeople who were not affiliated with government, Church or monarchy.

The Crusades provide a small taster of the atrocities and difficulties in any holy war, and perhaps a snapshot of what could happen during the End of Days.

The People's Crusade of 1096 is notable because of the involvement of many laypeople and pilgrims from throughout Europe. The numbers involved make this one of the largest disasters and losses of life during the Crusades, with Crusaders responsible for the deaths of thousands of Jews across Europe and, in turn, many of these Crusaders slaughtered by the more experienced Turkish soldiers.

What is notable about the People's Crusade is the anger and violence directed towards Jewish communities in Europe. As calls for Crusaders spread around Europe, the faithful directed their persecution towards the Jewish communities around the Rhineland in Germany. This violence led to the destruction of whole cities which had become Jewish settlements, and was, unfortunately, not the first time that this type of violence had been directed at the Jewish people.

Despite the numbers of Jews killed in their own homes and communities, there are many stories throughout Europe that try to elicit sympathy for the Crusaders themselves; even as they pillaged and invaded other countries, the Crusaders were portrayed as righteous and doing God's bidding. Perhaps the most interesting of these stories is the Children's Crusade, a Crusade that may not have even existed.

The stories of the Children's Crusade revolve around a group of faithful children who took it upon themselves to travel to the Holy Land, and the story is made all the more brutal by suggesting that most of these children fell to slavery, famine and the swords of the Byzantine Empire. The Children's Crusade supposedly began when a child prophet professed to receiving a message from Jesus and subsequently convinced his followers to travel with him to Jerusalem. The child even claimed that the Mediterranean Sea would part before them, meaning they did not need passage across the water.

In actual fact, this version of the Children's Crusade appears to be a combination of two separate stories:

♦   Stephan of Cloyes was a French shepherd boy who gathered a group of followers and claimed to have received a message from Jesus to be delivered to Philip II, the King of France. Stephan's pilgrimage to the king gradually gathered him followers, most of whom were vagabonds and beggars. However, the king refused an audience with Stephan and his followers quickly dispersed.

♦   Nicholas of Cologne tried to encourage a Children's Crusade but never actually left the European mainland. Travelling from Germany, Nicholas gathered an impressive bunch of followers, many of whom passed away while they crossed the Alps. When they reached the Mediterranean, they found that the seas did not part before them as Nicholas had promised.

Disappointed, most of them returned home, with some of the pilgrims settling locally in Genoa. Nicholas himself decided to return home but passed away en route. Meanwhile, back in Cologne, Nicholas' family were killed by neighbours whose children had followed him and subsequently been lost.

Despite the continued failures of the Crusades, the attempts to 'win back' the Holy Land continued into the fifteenth century and the Middle East continues to have political problems to the present day.

ST GEORGE AND THE DRAGON

One of the small benefits of the Crusades was an influx of Eastern goods and traditions back to the Holy Roman Empire and beyond, with those Crusaders who had survived bringing with them legends and stories from the Middle East.

One such story has had a lasting effect on the United Kingdom: St George and the Dragon. But even though St George has become the patron saint of Britain, his name borne by multiple kings and heirs, George's story does not come from Britain.

St George, or Georgius, was born in third-century Palestine and was a soldier in the Roman army at a time when Christians were still subject to persecution and death. Georgius was a respected soldier, and when the Emperor Diocletian ordered the death of every Christian in the Roman army, he was offered his life if he renounced his faith. When Georgius was subsequently sentenced to death, he donated all of his possessions and wealth to the poor.

Initially, Diocletian's plan was to kill off Christian influences within the military and elsewhere in the empire; instead, Georgius became a martyr, with his actions encouraging other Christians to profess their faith, and many other Roman citizens converting to Christianity to follow his example.

However, George's most lasting legacy is an adventure that may prove to be entirely fictional, in which Georgius comes face-to-face with a dragon-like beast that allows him to reaffirm his faith. The dragon that George faces is not as monstrous as some of the beasts of Revelations, but its role here cannot be ignored. The dragon is linked to a city of non-Christians and is ultimately defeated when the city converts to Christianity.

The city in question is Silene, a location that has long been lost, or perhaps known under another name – given the facts of Georgius' life and military service, Silene is likely to have been in northern Africa, potentially Libya.

Silene's dragon problem was not quite a dramatic *The Hobbit*-style affair: the dragon had simply set up beside the local lake, blocking the city's access to fresh water. In order to distract the dragon and retrieve water from the lake, the inhabitants of Silene would sacrifice a sheep to the dragon, fetching their water while the dragon ate.

When the people of Silene finally ran out of sheep, they turned to sacrificing maidens.

The story goes that George arrived in Silene just before the local princess was about to be sacrificed as the most recent distraction. George came to her rescue, wounding the dragon and leading it back towards the city. As the dragon moved closer, the citizens of Silene were obviously concerned, but George promised them that he would slay the dragon – if they converted to Christianity.

George's story appealed to the sensibilities of the Crusaders and the faithful at home in England: he became a hero because he bore witness to his religion, succeeded in converting an entire city to the faith and, ultimately, died for his beliefs.

Of course, George's triumph over the dragon also helped to cement him as a hero who had triumphed over a beast aligned with fire, similar in many ways to Revelations' depictions of Satan.

The gallant George and his protection of the princess' virtue also appealed to the popular story genre of Romance, with its tales about chivalrous knights and endangered maidens. In fact, even though he was long dead at the time, George is typically portrayed with the armour and heraldry of a knight of the Middle Ages rather than a soldier of the Roman Empire.

ZIONISM AND THE ORIGINS OF MODERN ISRAEL

Much of the political focus on the Middle East stems from the importance that all Abrahamic religions place on the area. Jerusalem is a site of great significance to all three religions, with pilgrimage to the area an important part of both the Jewish and Islamic faiths.

Although the Muslim pilgrimage, or *hajj*, traditionally brings its followers to Mecca, Jerusalem is nonetheless considered the third-holiest place in Islam as the home of the Al-Aqsa Mosque which was visited by Muhammad on his journey to Heaven. Control of

Jerusalem therefore grants political, religious and economic power: not only does a religion want to claim access to Jerusalem for their own faith, but a cynical reader might suggest that any claim to the city also gives access to the tourism routes that are a part of the pilgrimage process.

Jerusalem and its surrounding areas have been a hotly contested, occupied area since the time of the Bible. The area was part of the Roman Empire at the time of Jesus, falling under control of the Byzantine Empire until the sixteenth century. The Byzantine Empire was succeeded by the Ottoman Empire, and following that empire's collapse at the close of the First World War, the area fell under control of the British Empire.

For the Jewish faith, Jerusalem and Israel are the heart of lands promised to the Jewish people from the times of the Old Testament. Successive invasions and occupations have led to thousands of years during which this promise has not come to pass, leading many Jewish writers and philosophers to describe a great spiritual longing for the area.

Jerusalem is known as *Zion* in Hebrew, with Zionism becoming the name of this longing, and an associated movement involving the Jewish people's longed-for return to Israel, to build a Jewish nation there. Like many movements with their origins in any religion, Zionism has become increasingly political in a way that can no longer be viewed as exclusively religious.

The Zionist movement became popular towards the end of the nineteenth century as incidents of anti-Semitism became commonplace through Europe. Eastern Europe and the Russian Empire saw violent outbreaks against Jewish communities, with some states even expelling Jewish inhabitants.

The First Aliyah began in 1881 when a group of around 30,000 Jews migrated to Israel, under the control of Ottoman Palestine at the time. While there was always movement towards Jerusalem by various devout Jews, this was the largest single migration of people, and was followed by the Second Aliyah in 1904.

By the 1930s, over 200,000 Jews had migrated to Palestine, and with the rise of Nazism in Europe, a further 250,000 set out to relocate. By the middle of the 1940s, Jews accounted for nearly a third of the total population of Palestine.

In the wake of the Second World War, the Jewish population of the area started to rebel against British control, and in 1947 the British Empire announced its withdrawal from the area. The United Nations planned to divide the territory into three separate states: an Arab state, and a Jewish state, with Jerusalem an independent city-state that would govern itself. This proposal was accepted by the Jewish Agency, but the Arab League and Arab Higher Committee refused to agree.

Before any further discussions could take place, on 14 May 1948, Jewish leader David Ben-Gurion declared an independent Jewish State on land roughly corresponding to the classical boundaries of Israel, laying claim to some areas that were within the borders of neighbouring states. Seeing their claims to land challenged, these Arab countries declared war and invaded the new Israel.

Israel faced opposition from all sides, the world had seen enough wars in the early twentieth century and international pressure led to various ceasefires, although peace was never officially declared in the area. In fact, the State of Israel continues to face opposition from its neighbours and even within its own borders, with the Palestine Liberation Organisation fighting for independence from the Israeli government.

The area has remained in contention throughout the twentieth century and well into the twenty-first, with various international bodies getting involved in peace treaties or border negotiations. With the complex political climate of Israel and its neighbouring countries, there appears to be one certainty: if human conflict brings about the End of the World, it looks like politics will be forever involved in any religious conflict in this area.

PART 3

THE APOCALYPSE
THROUGH HISTORY

We've already seen how the story of Georgius the Roman soldier migrated to Britain, becoming an armour-wearing knight; similarly the role of religion began to become all the more important in the political sphere. The world was starting to become a much smaller place, but also a world with room for many different beliefs and interpretations.

The Middle Ages made way for the Age of Enlightenment and the Renaissance: in turn, these made way for the Age of Revolutions. Political, scientific and industrial changes swept the globe as humanity changed its focus from the gods above to the humanity within.

Where science and philosophy had been the domain of the nobility or clergy, new thoughts meant that these arts were respected and practised for their own sakes. As critical eyes looked at the world around us, eager to uncover its secrets, that same criticism was applied to both the human condition and our beliefs.

Despite the rise of humanism, religion was not forgotten: in fact, some of the great scientists and philosophers of this era were men of faith who used their critical eye to search for truth in the Bible and other holy books.

The effects of all these various revolutions, of humanism and development are still felt today: even in the twenty-first century, scientists, philosophers and theologians have different ideas about how and why the world will end. So far, none of them has come to pass.

The following are just some of these ideas.

10

CULTS,
SECTS AND
SCHISMS

Revelations and the End of the World were just one aspect of the Bible that humanism and science could look at. While Genesis provided ideas about the origins of both humanity and the world around us, Revelations suggested what might become of us.

Scientists looked at the events of Revelations, wondering if they could really occur, while philosophers focused on the dream-like nature of the Apocalypse and its hidden meanings. Even artists embraced the End of the World, with painters, sculptors and authors finding inspiration in imagery from both the Old and New Testaments.

This emphasis on the Endtimes led some Christian religious movements to focus on suffering and the religious enlightenment that could come from it, drawing inspiration from the life of Jesus. But stories like those of the sacrifice of Georgius, or the Old Testament hardships faced by Lot and Noah, gave further fuel to the fire.

Sin, and redemption, became important to these religious movements; different interpretations of Jesus' actions and writings led to different Churches, all operating under the umbrella of Christianity but with their own unique take on the Bible. And as these Churches moved further away from each other, familiar passages from the Bible developed new meanings.

This continued with the invention of the printing press in the fifteenth century, opening up the Bible to a new group of scholars.

These were people who had previously only heard words spoken or taught to them, relying on someone else's interpretations of the Bible's teachings. Now, not only was the Bible read by philosophers and scientists, by people who may not have practised the religion, but also learned men and women who brought experiences of commerce or law to their interpretations of the book.

Faith and religion became increasingly more personal, with smaller denominations and their beliefs proving as popular and enduring as larger Churches. In fact, even the core of Rome-based Christianity could not survive the various divisions of thought and interpretations, with the eleventh century seeing a schism that created the distinct Roman Catholic Church and Eastern Orthodox Church.

This set the stage for the European Reformation of the sixteenth century, which coincided with the formation of the offshoot Anglican Church under Henry VIII. Protestantism was born, laying the ground for further smaller fractions and differences in belief.

These new religious movements were very specifically based on the area and time in which they were born: the various Churches with their origins in the European Reformation have significantly different beliefs from the Anglican Church, which was mostly born out of Henry VIII's political and personal necessity.

And for each new Church there came a new take on the End of the World.

THE RAPTURE

The Rapture is a curious element of the Christian End of the World: it is almost exclusively spoken about within Protestant Churches, and nearly absent from Catholic beliefs.

The Rapture is first mentioned in the New Testament, specifically the First Letter to the Thessalonians. This book was written by Paul, one of Jesus' Twelve Apostles, and discusses what will happen after the Second Coming of Christ.

Paul suggests that as Jesus ascends to Heaven, humanity will be raised to meet him. To most Catholics, this is simply a reference to the resurrection of the dead in that all bodies rise again. However, some Protestant Churches have a very different interpretation of this.

The Puritan movement of the seventeenth century read this Rapture as a literal ascension of both the living and the dead: anyone who had led a virtuous life would be taken into Heaven alongside Jesus, with various depictions suggesting a sort of 'flight' into the heavens or a disappearance in a flash of light.

There is no definitive take on the Rapture, with different Churches suggesting it will occur before the events of the Apocalypse, meaning that the faithful will avoid the End of Days completely; others suggest that the Rapture will occur afterwards, and will be a reward for those who remained faithful through the final battles.

Regardless of the interpretation, the Second Coming is of key importance when it comes to the Rapture, with believers assuming that both are intertwined: if one should happen first, then the second stage will not be far behind.

One of the first – and best-known – historical figures to support the idea of the Rapture was Cotton Mather, a well-known American Puritan and key figure in the Salem Witch Trials. Mather predicted the Rapture to take place within his lifetime, putting forward multiple dates – obviously, none of them came to pass.

Although Mather died in 1728, many others have followed his example, predicting dates and suggestions for the Rapture and the End of the World; many Churches have adopted this as a key part of their beliefs, with the Rapture even extending to other offshoots of Christianity such as Jehovah's Witnesses and Mormons.

JEHOVAH'S WITNESSES

Although Jehovah's Witnesses only began practicing as a Church in the early nineteenth century, the religion traces its origins back to the Bible and a very specific date that suggests that the End of Days will occur very soon.

In fact, Jehovah's Witnesses believe that some of the earliest signs of the Endtimes have already come to pass.

Jehovah's Witnesses date the Babylonian invasion of Jerusalem, as featured in the Book of Daniel, to 607 BC and, working from there, they suggest that it is 2,520 years until the restoration of God's kingdom. Jehovah's Witnesses also believe that Jesus began his 1,000-year rule in Heaven in 1914, returning to Earth as a spirit at the same time. The warfare and conflict of the early twentieth century have only served to reinforce the belief, suggesting that these earthly conflicts echo a greater conflict in the heavens.

For Jehovah's Witnesses, this means that humanity is currently living through a period of tribulation in advance of Armageddon. During this period, all other religions will be eliminated, having misrepresented God in their teachings. This will make way for only the faithful to survive.

Jehovah's Witnesses believe that other events prophesied in Revelations have already come to pass, including the resurrection of 144,000 faithful who currently rule in Heaven as bishops and kings.

For this Church, the Endtimes are already here – we just need to wait for the next stage to happen.

THE CHURCH OF JESUS CHRIST OF LATTER-DAY SAINTS

Informally known as the Mormonism, the Church of Jesus Christ of Latter-Day Saints is based on the Book of Mormon, a sacred text written by several different prophets. Mormonism shares its origins with Judaism, Christianity and Islam, with the Book of Mormon acting as a supplement to the Bible. However, the former book's origins are firmly in the American continent.

Mormons believe that four tribes of Jewish people – Nephites, Jaredites, Mulekites and Lamanites – settled in the American continent during the times of the Old Testament. Separated from their homeland, these tribes nonetheless received their own versions of the prophecies and visitations that the faithful Jews received in Israel. These prophecies and events were written down and buried in what became modern New York.

One of the writers of the Book of Mormon, Moroni, appeared in the form of an angel to Joseph Smith in the early nineteenth century. He told Smith where to find the tablets that contained these teachings and how to translate them. The text became the Book of Mormon, outlining the history of these Jewish tribes after they left Israel. The book also suggests that, after the Bible's depiction of Jesus' ascension into Heaven, he then visited the Americas to repeat his teachings there and gather the different Jewish tribes in peace.

There is no scientific evidence that any elements of the Book of Mormon truly happened: DNA suggests that there are no common origins between the Jewish people and Native Americans, and Joseph Smith was notoriously secretive about the text of the Book of Mormon, refusing to allow anyone else to see or translate the writings. Some Mormons willingly accept this criticism of their religious text, questioning it as a truthful historical record, but still insist that Smith was divinely inspired, and this does not undermine their faith or the book's teachings.

Although Mormonism is practised internationally, there are aspects of the religion that are uniquely American, with Mormonism helping to lend the fledgling country a sense of purpose and history, rather than following beliefs with origins thousands of miles away. The religion has strong political and nationalist ties, with 2012 presidential candidate Mitt Romney and outspoken radio host Glenn Beck amongst the faithful. Mormons see themselves as playing an important part in spreading Christianity around the world, and a line can be seen connecting this with some elements of American foreign policy.

Joseph Smith supposedly referenced politics and the End of the World in his White Horse Prophecy. However, since this prophecy was not recorded or made public by Smith during his lifetime, it's possible that it was made by a follower who used Smith's name to gain more weight for his own views.

In this prophecy, Smith spoke about the American people migrating towards the Rocky Mountains and being seen as a white horse of peace and safety; the time would come when the US Constitution would hang by a thread, and the nation would be saved by the efforts of a white horse and a red horse coming together in its defence.

Some interpretations see a racial undertone to Smith's prophecy, with the US Constitution being saved only by white and 'red' – understood to mean Native American – peoples working together. However, the biblical association with the Four Horsemen cannot be ignored.

The Mormon Church does not make specific prophecies with regards to the date or time of the Apocalypse but, like Jehovah's Witnesses, they do believe that the Endtimes are imminent, with many current political events acting as a fulfilment of the biblical prophecies hinted at in Revelations.

ADVENTISM

In 1833, William Miller founded a new movement that saw the imminent Second Coming. Miller's beliefs came from a close reading of the Bible, and as he continued to study, he found further support for his ideas. A devout Baptist, Miller met with some scepticism when he made his discovery public, but as he revealed more about his method and the studies that he had undertaken, he gathered a following that spread around the world.

Like many predicted dates for the End of the World, Miller revised his figures a number of times. But he and his followers were convinced that one date in particular would be important for the Second Coming: 22 October 1844.

The Great Disappointment

Miller derived dates for the Second Coming from the Book of Daniel; with some complicated mathematics that converted the classical Jewish calendar to the modern Gregorian calendar, Miller arrived at the range of years during which the world would end.

He suggested that this would be between March 1843 and March 1844, but he would not be drawn on a more specific date.

Miller and his followers prepared for the end, but March 1844 came and went with no apocalyptic events. Miller pushed his date back by a month to April, but this also bore no fruit.

However, Samuel Snow, a colleague and friend of Miller, made further adjustments to the formula, narrowing down Miller's vague predictions and coming up with the specific date of 22 October.

Finally with a specific date to circle on their calendars, Millerites and Adventists began to take steps that they had only discussed until now, with many followers giving up their worldly possessions in preparation for the End of the World.

As you can probably guess by reading this book hundreds of years later, the world did not end on 22 October, with Miller and his faith becoming a point of ridicule around the world. Although Miller lost many followers, he continued to study the Bible and waited for the Second Coming until his own death in 1849.

The Bahá'i faith suggests that the arrival and declaration of the Báb coincides with this potential end, and may have fulfilled Miller's prophecy: the Báb first revealed himself in April 1844, and in October 1844 undertook a pilgrimage to Mecca where he made his announcement public.

THE STRANGE CASE OF JOANNA SOUTHCOTT

Joanna Southcott was born in 1750 in Devon and spent her life working as a housemaid and farm worker. Around the age of 50, Joanna began to receive visions which she believed to be prophecies sent from God. After some of her minor prophecies came true, Joanna's writings were adopted by a small group of believers, with Joanna becoming a minor celebrity.

In 1814, at 64 years of age, Joanna announced that she was four months pregnant. As a virgin who had never married, Joanna believed that her pregnancy was a gift from God and that her child would be the Second Coming of Jesus Christ – it was not difficult to convince her followers of that same fact. Joanna even wrote about some of the symptoms of her pregnancy, describing in great detail the movements within her womb as she grew to a large size.

After Southcott had gone well past term, she came to believe that Jesus Christ would not be born to an unmarried woman. Replicating the family of Jesus, Mary and Joseph, Joanna married one of her followers, John Smith, with an agreement that the marriage would be annulled if the child was not born.

Southcott passed away in December 1814, supposedly fourteen months pregnant, with no sign of any child. An autopsy was held on her corpse, attended by several followers and medical doctors. No sign of pregnancy was found. Instead, Joanna's abdomen had swollen to nearly four times the usual size thanks to a build-up of fat and gas.

With no sign of a Second Coming, her followers disbanded, suitably deflated that the End of the World had not come to pass.

11

PORTENTS OF THE END: NOSTRADAMUS AND PROPHECIES

NOSTRADAMUS

Michel de Nostradame, known by the pen-name Nostradamus, is a notorious figure when discussing the End of the World, and no book discussing the Apocalypse would be complete without referencing him.

Born in France in the early sixteenth century, Nostradamus was an apothecary – a posh, old-fashioned name for a chemist – and seer. After years of studying and practicing medicine, Nostradamus published his first almanac in 1550, collecting a number of predictions that he had previously made. He published the book under the Latinised version of his own name, the sixteenth-century equivalent of the heavy-metal umlaut. Some of these predictions were specific, involving weather or crops, others were significantly vaguer.

This almanac sold so successfully that Nostradamus was encouraged to write more, publishing over 6,000 prophecies and star charts. He also entered into correspondence with dignitaries and nobles, both from his native France and internationally, creating personalised star charts and predictions for them and their families.

One such noblewoman to embrace Nostradamus – or perhaps respond in fear to the fact that such prophecies existed – was Catherine de Medici, the wife of King Henry II of France. Nostradamus initially feared for his life when contacted by Catherine, but she was so convinced by his prophetic words that she hired him as the family's personal physician.

Fearing repercussions from both the Crown and the Church, Nostradamus adopted a sort of code for his prophecies, which became similar to the Book of Revelations: by using Latin, Greek and other contemporary languages, Nostradamus hid his own meanings. While it kept Nostradamus alive, it also meant that his predictions could apply to multiple things at once and were usually only attributed as correct after an occurrence that fulfilled them.

In 1555, Nostradamus published another book of prediction, called *Les Propheties* or *The Prophecies*. He took this opportunity to downplay the involvement of any 'magic' or occultism in his predictions. Instead, he associated historic events with the positions and alignments of the planets and stars, suggesting that similar events would occur again when the planets were next in a similar position.

This made Nostradamus one of the first people to apply a scientific approach to prophecies and the End of the World, but he certainly was not the last: science and faith would continue to intertwine, creating new approaches to religion that bordered on the occult.

Nostradamus' prophecies were condemned by both contemporary scientists and clergy, but the legacy of his work has lasted to the present day, and readers have suggested that he predicted the French revolution, the rise of Hitler, the atomic bomb and the 9/11 terrorist attack on the World Trade Center.

Nostradamus' prophecies are curiously quiet on the End of the World, however – or rather very few interpretations point towards a definite series of events leading to it. But perhaps these will only be discussed after the Endtimes have happened.

Some conspiracy theories suggest that there is a Cult of Nostradamus, possessing secret knowledge of these prophecies, either holding some key to translating them or possessing some predictions that have not been made public.

This cult supposedly uses this knowledge to manipulate events in their own favour; as befitting any conspiracy theory, political leaders and businessmen are rumoured to be amongst the most senior members of the cult.

As with the best conspiracy theories, there's little proof that the Cult of Nostradamus exists, but if you look for it hard enough, you could probably convince yourself that it's true.

Nostradamus' reputation is not limited to poetic verses, as a number of abstract paintings are also named after him, the *Vaticinia Nostradami*. The paintings were found with a covering letter that suggested they were inspired by Nostradamus, but examination suggests that they are actually older.

The paintings feature surreal imagery and symbols of saints and beasts, similar to those discussed in Revelations. The content of the *Vaticinia Nostradami* is also similar to the Chinese *Tui bei tu*, an illustrated poem that features similar prophecies.

THE PROPHECY OF THE POPES

Although St Patrick is the patron saint of Ireland, he wasn't born there – like Georgius, Patrick is the patron saint of a nation to which he was not born. Unlike Georgius, Patrick actually did spend most of his life in Ireland after being born in Britain – probably Wales or Cumbria.

Instead, the first native Irishman to be conferred with sainthood was Saint Malachy, Archbishop of Armagh from approximately 1132 to 1137. Centuries after Malachy's death, the Prophecy of the Popes was published by a Benedictine monk, Arnold Wion. It's unclear if the prophecy was attributed to Malachy or if Wion simply used Malachy's name on his own prediction – as with Nostradamus' Latinised name, he could avoid repercussions by blaming someone else.

The prophecy consists of 112 short Latin phrases, with each verse dedicated to a different pope, and it also suggests that these 112 popes provide a sort of countdown to the Last Judgement, which will coincide with the final pope.

Like Nostradamus' predictions, most of the Prophecy of the Popes can be manipulated after the fact and interpreted in different ways – most of the prophecies only make sense after the next pope has come to power. As if to prove the point, many of the earliest verses describe their corresponding popes in great detail, including facts about their early lives and places of birth; on the other hand, later entries are brief and vague.

However, the Prophecy of the Popes is one to pay close attention to: Pope Francis, elected to the Papacy in March 2013, is the 112th pope on this list. As of writing this book, it remains to be seen whether he will be the '*Petrus Romanus*', who reigns over the Church during the Endtimes.

CHRISTOPHER COLUMBUS

Columbus is best known as an explorer, the captain responsible for the 'discovery' of the American continent in 1492. Of course, the importance placed on Columbus neglects that the continent had been inhabited for thousands of years, by both natives and Norse colonists.

But Columbus also made his own small contribution to the wealth of apocalyptic literature: he wrote and published his *Book of Prophecies* in the early years of sixteenth century.

In this book, Columbus sets out four things that he believed would herald the End of the World:

- ◆ Christianity would spread across the world.
- ◆ The Garden of Eden would be re-discovered.
- ◆ A final Crusade would win back Jerusalem.
- ◆ The Last Roman Emperor would be appointed, a figure who would stand alongside the Messiah and lead his earthly armies.

THE LAST ROMAN EMPEROR

Columbus' reference to the Last Roman Emperor suggests that he was aware of a much older prophecy: this figure is not mentioned in Revelations, but is part of other texts that supplement the Christian belief in the Endtimes.

The prophecy of the Last Roman Emperor is first mentioned in the *Apocalypse of Pseudo-Methodius*, written in the seventh century which, like Revelations, uses a dream about the End of the World to reveal some truths to its writer.

This may have been adapted from an older pagan prophecy, attributed to the Tiburtine Sibyl in the days of Greek and Roman mythology, which predicts a ruler who would come to unite humanity.

A sibyl was a seer and wise woman in classical Greek and Roman society, and regularly features in literature from this period; often, the sibyl would speak a seemingly innocent prophecy that would then come true in some horrific manner, despite the subject's attempts to avoid it.

The Greeks also loved their irony, and many of the sibyls and prophets were blind, or their prophecies held some other loophole. Oedipus was prophesied to kill his own father and marry his mother. Adopted by a neighbouring family, Oedipus became aware of the prophecy and fled his adopted family – only to return to the city of his birth and there fulfil the prophecy.

Similarly, the prophetess Cassandra warned about the events of the Trojan War, but her predictions fell on deaf ears after she was cursed for spurning the advances of Apollo.

The global decline of empires and monarchy means that the prophecy of the Last Roman Emperor has become rather outdated and fallen out of fashion. But it is nonetheless combined with the Prophecy of the Popes – with the Pope also known as Emperor of Rome – and indicates that the final pope may indeed be considered as the Last Roman Emperor.

12

BRITAIN AND THE APOCALYPSE

Britain was in a unique position during the Age of Enlightenment: the British Empire was active in the world, with access to scholars and centres of learning across the globe. However, the heart of the empire was still removed from mainland Europe, unaffected by some of the political and cultural changes that swept across the continent.

Britain instead faced its own challenges, with the End of the World being viewed through the lens of the nation's artistic, political and military exploits – in most cases, the British Empire was the victor and aggressor, the holder of power in most dealings. This vision persisted as the empire continued to grow, incorporating influences from within and further afield.

PRE-1600

Beowulf

While the stories of classical Greece and Rome were embraced by British Romantic poets for their chivalry and heroism, *Beowulf* is part of the same tradition – just coming from a little further north. One of the defining works of Norse mythology, the story of Beowulf came to our shores across the North Sea, bringing with it tales of savage Vikings and victory over monsters.

The epic poem details Beowulf's struggle against the monsters threatening his village, first the monstrous Grendel and then Grendel's mother. After Beowulf defeats them both, he returns home to rule his village for fifty successful years – until his village is threatened by a dragon. Beowulf slays this beast after a glorious battle, but the struggle leads to his own injury and death.

The presence of the dragon draws comparison with Revelations, with Beowulf appearing as a Messianic figure that ensures the safety of his people – in this case, his villagers. His fifty-year reign is even comparable to the rule of Jesus: both occur between two separate battles, and both signal a time of peace and prosperity.

There is no definite source or date for the poem, so it can only be guessed whether *Beowulf* was inspired by Christianity or developed separately. However, some other Old English poets and writers were no stranger to Christian imagery: *The Dream of the Rood* features a dream-like vision as the writer contemplates the cross upon which Jesus was killed. Like Jesus, the cross is subsequently resurrected and proceeds to reign as the greatest of all trees.

Domesday Book

Domesday Book – or Doomsday in modern English – was the result of a large-scale survey of the British Isles carried out in the eleventh century at the the command of William the Conqueror. Having taken the English throne, William was especially interested in the exact size of his new kingdom and the income he could assure by levying taxes.

Domesday Book consists of two separate works: an in-depth survey of Norfolk, Essex and Sussex; and a less-extensive survey of Durham, Westmoreland, Cumberland and Northumberland. The book drew up the borders of land and property, a one-stop solution to all land disputes and arguments over taxation. In all cases, Domesday Book was final and people could not appeal against its judgements.

So how did it get its name?

Domesday Book was likened to the Book of Judgement, the scroll with seven seals that features so prominently in Revelations: like Domesday Book, this scroll represented a final authority for humanity that could not be appealed.

THE SEVENTEENTH CENTURY

Milton's Paradise Lost

First published in 1667, John Milton's epic poem *Paradise Lost* sets out to 'justify the ways of God to men'. The work traces the biblical story of creation, moving through the revolt and subsequent fall of Satan.

Milton's work is a massively important piece of literature in its characterisation of Satan, applying some very human personalities onto the divine forces that could bring about the End of the World. *Paradise Lost* paints Satan as a tragic hero, a character brimming with pride and whose downfall is ultimately caused by his own actions. While Satan remains the enemy of God and the villain of the piece, his motivations and actions are human and relatable: he is shown winning many followers with his passionate – and in most cases, reasonable – arguments.

Satan's most famous quote still lingers in popular culture: 'Better to reign in Hell, than serve in Heav'n'. The quote gives us some interesting insight into how the forces of evil, whether divine or human, feel about the concept of political power, both in having it, and in being subject to it.

Shakespeare's The Tempest

Most of Shakespeare's plays indulge in some form of magic or magical imagery, whether it's the witches and prophecy of *Macbeth*, the love potion of *A Midsummer Night's Dream* or the supposed living statue of *Othello*. But in *The Tempest* Shakespeare actually takes a magician as his hero: Prospero was previously the Duke of Milan, but has been deposed, his political power stolen from him. The play concerns

Prospero's plan to destroy the men who have ruined him and restore his daughter to her rightful place in the kingdom.

The Tempest is the final play attributed to Shakespeare, and many scholars treat it as a retrospective of his work, focusing either on Shakespeare's biography – drawing similarities between the playwright and Prospero – or the theatricality of the play and its fantastical imagery.

With Prospero acting as a proud deposed ruler, there are many similarities between him and Milton's Satan: both are not just deposed, but also obsessed with the notion of power, and both seek to deliver their own versions of justice. Prospero summons the tempest of the title which leads to a shipwreck; the existence of the storm proves that Prospero possesses otherworldly powers – and corrupt reasons for using them – which could ally him to characters with the forces of evil during Armageddon.

That Prospero, who brings about this destruction, is an individual not a force or a movement, gives us some insight into the representation of the Antichrist as we move towards the modern world. As the End of the World becomes significantly more political, could the Endtimes be brought about by a single man or woman who has been corrupted by political power? And just where could this individual get such power?

Hobbes' Leviathan

Taking its name from the biblical Leviathan, a sea creature from the Old Testament, Thomas Hobbes' 1651 book is a significant part of political and social thought. *Leviathan* reflects on government and society and how the two interact, a sort of update of Plato's *Republic* for a more modern world.

Hobbes sees humanity as a chaotic force that will constantly work against any government or other means of control, ultimately leading to failure. In order to minimise this resistance, Hobbes believes that political control should come from a single individual source: he considers monarchy to be the best form of government, as it eliminates the ability for society to resist.

Hobbes then sees religion as a public indulgence: he suggests that the authority of the Church does not come from a divine insight, but rather an agreement amongst the people to support it. Karl Marx would later describe religion as the 'opium of the people', a sort of ultimate distraction from which people gather comfort and a sense of community, but nothing else.

Hobbes' near-atheist views extended to the End of the World too, and the final section of *Leviathan* is dedicated to what he calls the 'Kingdom of Darkness'. This is not an earthly or physical kingdom, but rather the darkness formed by human ignorance and the misinterpretation of religious texts. Hobbes creates a complicated argument that, ultimately, suggests that religion and government have no connection and should be kept distinct and separate.

Finally, Hobbes suggests that all human conflict stems from a fear of the *summum malum*, or death: as humanity seeks to avoid its own death, it causes destruction and violence that could even bring about the End of the World. But Hobbes does have one suggestion: this fear could be controlled and manipulated by rulers for their own ends.

To Hell or to Connaught

The biblical imagery of the Four Horsemen reared its head once more in the seventeenth century, when Oliver Cromwell led a Parliamentary invasion of Ireland in order to combat resistance to British rule. The Cromwellian Conquest cemented British control over the island and has had repercussions that can still be felt today.

Cromwell's role in British history is well documented, and he is mostly respected within Britain. But the Irish invasion paints him as a wholly monstrous figure, scouring the country on horseback and driving the populace from their homes and towards the inhospitable west coast – the province of Connaught.

Although the Four Horsemen are not referenced directly, Cromwell and other conquerors of the time are depicted similarly to the first horseman of the Apocalypse, especially by the peoples that they were conquering; after conquistador activity wiped out South American natives, art and imagery shows the invading forces rearing on horseback, ready to trample on the natives.

Interestingly, in another link that ties Cromwell to the Endtimes, one of Cromwell's close advisors – and holder of the title of Secretary of Foreign Tongues in his Parliament – was poet and writer of *Paradise Lost*, John Milton.

The Fifth Monarchists

Taking their name from a reference in the Book of Daniel, the Fifth Monarchy Men were an organisation formed in 1649, who believed that the Apocalypse would occur within the next

few decades. Specifically, they believed that the year 1666 would bring about the End of Days by combining the 1,000 years that Satan would spend in the pit with the number of the Beast.

The Fifth Monarchists were formed in the wake of the complex political landscape of seventeenth-century Britain where Charles I had been deposed and Britain flirted with the idea of becoming a parliamentary democracy. This was seen as the end of the British Empire, the fourth empire that must end before Jesus would build his fifth empire on Earth.

The Great Plague of London

Distance from Europe is not always a bad thing: while the United Kingdom may have been left out of some of the dramatic events of the Middle Ages, it also escaped the clutches of the Black Death, which swept across the continent in the fourteenth century.

But this was only delaying the inevitable, with the Great Plague making its way to London in 1665; with its arrival, several writers likened it to the biblical plagues of the Old Testament.

The plague was transmitted by flea bites from infected rats, a common occurrence in the London of the time. The infection then led to the growth of boils and pustules around the neck and other lymph nodes, with gangrene causing the death of other bodily organs. This gangrene would cause skin and tissues to turn black, especially on the extremities of fingers and toes, earning the disease's nickname of the Black Plague.

By the seventeenth century, conditions had improved enough that the plague was no longer as deadly as it once was. But it still proved to be a death sentence to Londoners living in poor and squalid conditions.

Estimates suggest that the Black Plague was responsible for the death of around 40 per cent of the total population of Europe during the fourteenth and fifteenth centuries. When it landed in London in 1665, the plague killed over 100,000 people, but it is possibly responsible for much more: diarist Samuel Pepys suggested that the clerks of London were overwhelmed by the reported deaths during the period, and the figures for actual deaths could be nearly 30 per cent higher than those recorded.

While London's overall death toll was lower than that of the earlier continental outbreaks, this strain of the disease still proved to be particularly infectious, with carriers falling to the disease very quickly; the Black Plague struck a London that was not prepared, and had no real idea how to deal with such a crisis.

Some people preached that the plague was sent from God to cleanse the city, and with the symptoms of the disease, it was a justifiable argument. The swelling of the lymph nodes meant pustules and growths around the crotch, and with the disease being especially prevalent around the 'unclean' portions of the city, those commentators linked the plague to the presence of sin.

The Great Plague of London was not alone in its apocalyptic effects on the city. However, as plague landed on London's streets, fire was just a little bit behind.

The Great Fire of London

The phrase 'cleansing fire' is usually used in a religious context, with the notion that flames will destroy sins and purify the people. However, this proved to be a very beneficial case for the London of September 1666.

On the night of the 2 September, a fire started in a bakery on Pudding Lane that quickly spread to neighbouring buildings. At a time of timber construction, there was ample fuel for the fire to spread.

Firefighting measures of the time focused on destroying buildings to stop the fire's growth, rather than quenching existing flames. But this dramatic method of destroying the fire's path was not enacted as quickly as needed. Because of the destruction to homes and businesses, London's Lord Mayor, Thomas Bloodworth, was slow to act. That the fire had started in the middle of the night also meant that it had already grown to a significant blaze before the authorities were called on to address it directly.

The fire raged across the city for three days, only dying out on 5 September; as a result of both the fire and the attempts to contain it, over 1,000 buildings were destroyed. Nearly 100 of these buildings were churches, and St Paul's Cathedral was counted among the fatalities.

The Great Fire had an unexpected up-side, however: by September 1666, the tail-end of the Great Plague was still simmering through parts of London, and the fire is credited with eliminating the last remnants of the disease.

The year of the Great Fire of London should not be ignored, and some of the citizens' more fanciful ideas suggested that this was, in fact, part of the End of Days, thanks to the year containing the number of the Beast.

13

NEWTON, NUMBERS AND SECRET MESSAGES

While the United Kingdom was not as directly affected by the Renaissance as mainland Europe, it was a key player in a different sort of revolution.

The scientific revolution is not a clearly defined movement, nor is it limited to a specific time or place: it is instead a catch-all phrase to describe the leaps and bounds of scientific discovery that formed the basis of the modern world. The expression was first coined in 1939, referring to the time between the 1500 and 1800: although scientific advancements continued well past 1800, most of our later discoveries are based on knowledge that was uncovered during this period.

The scientific revolution also meant some interesting interactions between science and religion. We've already looked at how philosophers such as Nostradamus used code in order to avoid behaviour that could be seen as heretical, but he was not alone. The Roman Catholic Church placed limits on what European scientists were allowed to investigate, and many discoveries were oppressed or hidden, as they challenged the faith of the Church.

That is not to say that all scientists turned their back on religion: in fact, some of the most interesting scientific developments of this period were discovered by men who continued to practise their faith.

GALILEO GALILEI

Galileo Galilei was born in Pisa in February 1564 and became one of the foremost scientists in the field of early physics. Some of Galileo's theories have since been disproved, but those same theories provided something to be challenged and interrogated. However, he is probably best remembered as one of the first men to experience first-hand the struggle between science and faith, and to face the consequences of that battle.

Galileo and his scientific endeavours were found guilty of heresy and placed under house arrest in 1633, but the main contributing factor to this conviction was not due to Galileo's own discoveries. Galileo was an ardent supporter of Copernicus and his theory that the Earth was round and revolved around the sun; this contradicted the religious belief that the universe revolved around the Earth. By supporting and teaching Copernicus' theories, as well as using them as the basis of his own work, Galileo ran afoul of the authorities in his staunchly religious native Italy.

Since Galileo's death, the controversy of his life has become a talking point for Vatican authorities: while his work was officially removed from the list of banned books in 1835, his is still a complicated legacy. Pope John Paul II expressed regret over how the Church originally handled Galileo and his teachings, but his successor, Pope Benedict XVI, suggested that the reaction to Galileo was an appropriate reaction of the time that cannot be judged by modern standards of reason.

But even as his discoveries challenged the faith of the Church, Galileo did not turn his back on religion. In fact, he and other scientists like Leonardo da Vinci and Isaac Newton cast their scientific studies towards the world of religion and faith as well, all to help better understand the world around them, where it had come from and where it could be going.

LEONARDO DA VINCI

Leonardo da Vinci is better known as an artist than a scientist, but during his lifetime, neither was an exclusive discipline. Da Vinci sought to better understand the natural sciences so as to improve his art, with much of his studies focusing on anatomy and architecture. Da Vinci was also an inventor, whose scientific endeavours were surprisingly ahead of their time.

There is no evidence to link Da Vinci directly with the End of the World, but fictional works of the twentieth century have made him a key player, possessing secret knowledge about the Endtimes.

Dan Brown's novel *The Da Vinci Code* suggests that Da Vinci was part of a secret society, the Priory of Sion, that was trusted with the hidden truths of the Catholic Church, and that there are clues to these secrets throughout the body of his work.

Brown's book had a significant cultural impact, giving further credence to a conspiracy theory that the works of the past might contain religious truths and help to provide illumination on Revelations and the End of the World.

The Priory of Sion

Papal documents from the twelfth century mention a small monastic order in Mount Zion in Jerusalem, literally a priory. This is the only factual account of any such order with official ties to the Catholic Church.

However, *The Da Vinci Code* seems to take its inspiration from a slightly different source, namely a twentieth-century French society with notions of grandeur.

Under French law, a society of any sort needs to be registered, and the Priory of Sion was registered in 1956 under the name of Pierre Plantard. The paperwork showed that the Priory of Sion indicated that it would be a semi-religious organisation, a sort of charity/ outreach programme working in the community. The organisation was dissolved in that same year, although it was revived multiple times throughout the remainder of the twentieth century.

Plantard concocted an intricate backstory for the order, claiming that it was descended from this Jerusalem-based Abbey of Our Lady of Mount Zion, and that both the abbey and the order had been founded by the pope himself.

Through forged documents and paper-thin historical connections, Plantard claimed to be descended from Dagobert II, a seventh-century king of central Europe. Through Dagobert, Plantard claimed that he was the fulfilment of Nostradamus' predicted Great Monarch, a figure equivalent to the Last Roman Emperor.

Plantard's claims have been widely debunked multiple times, usually stemming from his own overeager claims of authenticity. In 1993, for example, Plantard claimed that recently deceased millionaire Roger-Patrice Pelat was a member of his secret society. However, in a turn of events that Plantard could not have foreseen, Pelat's fortunes and death were under investigation for a conspiracy all their own, involving the apparent suicide of former French Prime Minister Pierre Bérégovoy. Plantard's claims dragged him into the investigation, and when he was brought before the courts, he was forced to admit that most of his documentation and claims had been forged.

ISAAC NEWTON

Isaac Newton is a name more closely associated with science class than religion or history, but for a man born in 1642, he has had a surprisingly large influence on the modern world. Newton's studies laid the foundation for modern physics: not only did he formulate universal laws such as gravity and energy, but he also did the basic mathematics that made all manner of mechanical devices possible.

Newton was also a man of faith, and he is known to have devoted much of his free time to the mathematical theory of the Bible, searching for hidden meanings in its pages. He did enough research that he even had his own opinions on how the world would end.

Newton was born into an Anglican family, but his early relationships with religion were not amiable: his father had passed away, and when his mother re-married a clergyman, Newton was left to the care of his grandmother. Newton attended university at Cambridge, and would have been required to join the priesthood after he completed his studies – several accounts suggest that Newton considered dropping out of college to avoid this outcome. However, there was no deadline to this ordination, and Newton succeeded in avoiding this fate by postponing taking any vows until he finally received special dispensation directly from King Charles II.

Despite his seeming lack of interest in religious life, Newton committed himself to the study of the Bible. He had an interesting theory about its contents and the writings of classical philosophers and scientists: he believed that the Bible contained great truths and enlightenment but these messages had been lost in time. After centuries of subsequent translations, each of which would have been subtly influenced by the intentions of the translators, this enlightenment was no longer visible in the contemporary Bible.

With no small amount of pride, Newton considered himself to be divinely inspired to understand the messages within the Bible's pages and that only he and a few select others could lift the veil of ignorance that hung over its contents. Newton's work in this field appears to have been motivated by pride rather than any concern about the End of Days; in fact, Newton even acknowledged that if and when he was able to completely understand the Bible, its contents may not be truly and completely understood until after any prophesied events had taken place.

Using knowledge of classical numerology and architecture, Newton developed an interpretation of the dates and years within the Bible where each 'day' corresponded to a year, all the while paying specific attention to the calendars used by those who wrote and compiled the Bible. While Newton disagreed with the practice of specifying dates for the Apocalypse, he instead pointed towards a range of dates, suggesting that the End of Days described in the Bible would not occur any earlier than 2060, nor any later than 2370.

However, Newton never made these speculations public, and they come to us through scrawled notes discovered in the early twenty-first century and attributed to Newton. While the notes outline Newton's method at arriving at these dates, there is no corroborating evidence that these were meant to be anything other than theories or partial deductions that would have formed a part of a bigger picture.

Like Leonardo da Vinci, the stories that grew around Newton's diverse interests have been manipulated through time, and popular culture and conspiracy theories also associate Newton with secret orders and societies.

Chief amongst these societies was the Rosicrucians, a network of scientists and philosophers who, like Newton, looked to classical texts and their writers as possessors of mystical knowledge. With a name derived from the imagery of a red – or bloody – cross, the Rosicrucians believed that, by combining religious imagery with the classical sciences, they could achieve enlightenment.

There is no evidence that Newton was a member of this order, nor that the order truly existed, but the story of its creation has spawned many other tales, and even more imitators.

14

SECRETS AND REVOLUTIONS

The late eighteenth century triggered a period of political instability across the world, due in no small part to the scientific and philosophical learning of the Age of Enlightenment. This knowledge had a direct

effect on political thoughts and theories, lending confidence and authority to elements of society that had previously been oppressed.

GEORGE WASHINGTON AND THE AMERICAN REVOLUTION

After years of British rule, the seeds of nationalism and independence began to grow in America in the mid-eighteenth century. At the forefront of the American movement for independence was George Washington, a man whom popular culture has tied to as many secret societies as Newton and Leonardo da Vinci.

Washington was definitely a man of Christian faith, but his religious affiliations are still speculated about: during his life, Washington attended services and sermons at many different churches of many different denominations. But one thing is common: Washington did not take communion at any of them.

However, the associations between Washington and secret societies are not as spurious as with Newton or da Vinci: Washington was initiated into the Freemasons in 1752 and was appointed Master of the Virginia Lodge in 1788.

FREEMASONS: A SOCIETY WITH SECRETS

Freemasonry has its origins in the fourteenth century. There is no definitive written history of public record, but it is believed to have the same origins as European trade guilds. These guilds were initially groups of craftsmen providing mutual training and support, as well as confirming a certain standard of their work.

Local organisations of Freemasons are known as Lodges, with mutual membership and recognition of others. In an age before social media, travelling Freemasons could be welcomed at the local Lodge and expect to find acquaintances and lodgings there.

The Freemasons are also heavily involved in local community and charity. Although they maintain a public front, the organisation itself remains impenetrable to the common man, and as befits any such organisation, an air of mystery has grown around the Freemasons and their members.

The Freemasons themselves are not a hidden society: the location of Lodges is openly known – especially those of grand design – and much of their imagery and symbolism is transparent, including a great emphasis on religious, mathematical and architectural symbolism.

Freemasons are quick to suggest that they are not a secret society, but rather that there are elements of the society that they choose to keep private from non-members. As a result, stories and legends have developed around the idea of Freemasonry. Some of this has taken the form of anti-Masonic propaganda, suggesting that the Freemasons are involved in secret plots to rule the world.

The Anti-Masonic Party was formed in America in 1828 as a political movement firmly opposed to the spread of Freemasonry and its teaching. Although the party only existed for a decade, it raised enough questions about the Freemasons, their secret beliefs and their methodologies that a stigma has been associated with their name ever since.

Freemason Albert Pike, a well-known American confederate and attorney, highlighted the links between Freemasonry and ancient mysteries; while this could be seen as merely boastful, or even an attempt to explain Freemasonry without disclosing its secrets, this was taken by the Anti-Masonic Party and other rivals as an indication that the society was allied with pagan or Satanic worship. In actual fact, the ancient mysteries discussed by Pike are probably the same mathematical and universal orders embraced by Newton.

As with any society operating in secret, conspiracy theories have suggested that the Freemasons are the public face of the Illuminati and are pivotal players in global politics. In truth, Freemasonry is not a religion, and there are no public writings or theories on the End of the World. The society has members from all religions and ethnic denominations, placing great importance on an individual's faith and the honour and truth descending from that.

THE ILLUMINATI AND THE NEW WORLD ORDER

Most of the conspiracy theories relating to secret societies have a common root: they are linked to the concept of the Illuminati, a secret society in their own right who use Freemasons, Rosicrucians and other orders as a front to their far more sinister and dastardly organisation. There is no proof that the Illuminati exist, but like other orders, they have their origins in very real history.

The historical Illuminati were founded by Adam Weishaupt in 1776 at the University of Ingolstadt in Bavaria. The society was modelled on the structure of the Freemasons, with the aim of promoting education and liberal thinking, eliminating superstition and doing away with the tight religious hold over politics and education.

Because of its radical ideas, the group operated in a sort of secret capacity, constantly under the threat of being condemned for heresy or treason. This organisation was outlawed and disbanded by royal decree in 1777, though two different books published only decades later claimed that the society was still functioning and had been largely responsible for the events behind the French Revolution.

This rumour was quite popular at the start of the nineteenth century, with further myths and legends suggesting that the Illuminati were also involved in the American Revolution, the Great Fire of London and other large-scale political events or disasters. Even as rational men spoke out about the unlikelihood that such an organisation could exist, these statements created a self-perpetuating cycle, taken as being nothing more than the society's attempts to cover its own tracks.

These theories and conspiracies have continued into the twenty-first century, with suggestions that the Illuminati continue to exert great power over international governments, even possessing advanced technology that allow them to trigger earthquakes or tornadoes. In this age of mass media, any event that is not wholly understood can be blamed on this secret society and its mysterious ways.

Believers suggest that the Illuminati are manipulating events as they work towards the creation of a New World Order, a unified worldwide government; if the Endtimes of Revelations involve all of humanity uniting under one leader, any movement towards a worldwide government appears to be hastening that Armageddon. This theory is by no means the largest resistance to the United Nations and the European Union, but it should not be forgotten when patriots argue for sovereign rule.

The phrase 'new world order' was first coined in the wake of the First World War, and was a legitimate reference to the existence of the League Of Nations: the League had been formed in the wake of global warfare, recognising the growing need for international politics to look at a bigger, worldwide picture. While the League of Nations was never meant to lead to a new world government, some of its opponents still resisted the power that any organisation like this would have over member nations.

The phrase 'new world order' was used by US President Woodrow Wilson and by Winston Churchill, seeping into popular consciousness. Later, the phrase was used by H.G. Wellls as the title for his book *The New World Order*. In this book, Wells outlined his theories for a government that could span the entire world: it is a non-fictional discussion of how this government could work, similar to Plato's *Republic* or Moore's *Utopia*.

In the years since publication, it's been suggested that this book was written after Wells uncovered some secret truths behind the Illuminati and the New World Order; of course, he is not the only

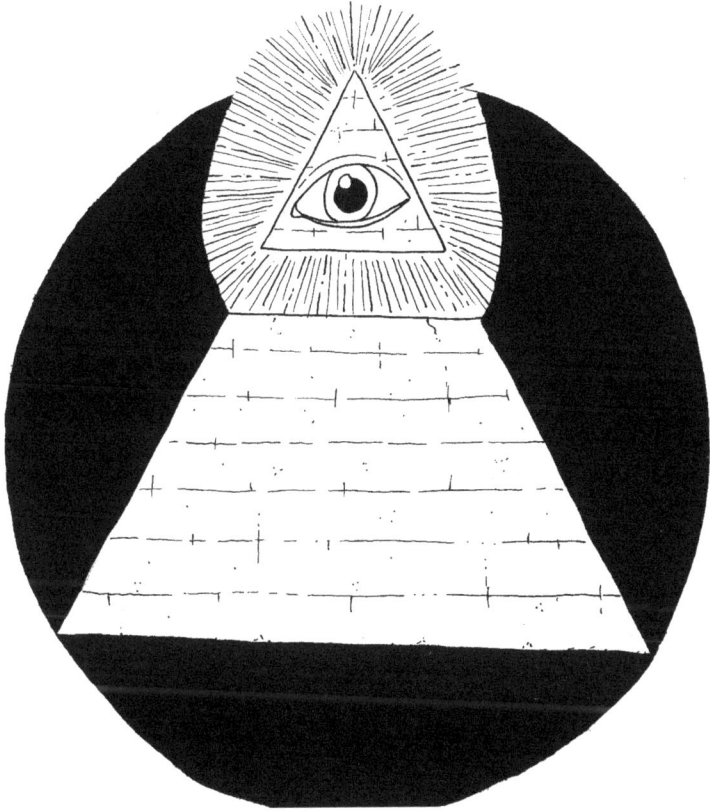

science-fiction writer of the twentieth century whose ideas have been taken as gospel truth.

One of the key parts of Wells' imagined future is the increasingly large role of corporations and industry: as bigger multinational companies operate on a global basis, various parties look towards their influence on all types of government as a negative factor.

The conspiracies involving the Illuminati are so varied that they would require their own book to discuss fully. But if you fear for the coming Apocalypse and are looking for a group to blame, open season has been declared on the Illuminati for centuries.

THE FRENCH REVOLUTION: A CASE STUDY IN DYSTOPIA

The year 1789 saw the first rumblings of the French Revolution, one of the definitive movements that signalled the end of an age of empires and monarchy. Unfortunately, as empires died, new movements grew that would seek to take their place.

As France experienced the depths of an economic crisis, the nobility remained unaffected. With stories of famine and starvation on the streets of Paris, Queen Marie-Antoinette is famously reputed to have said 'Let them eat cake'. The queen's words have been interpreted in several different ways: mostly, it is seen as a naive comment that only highlights the monarchy's failings and inadequate home economics, but others suggest that Marie-Antoinette may have had the makings of a royal heroine, wanting to share the royal coffers and larders with the poorer souls on the streets, but facing resistance from the rest of the court.

The French Revolution was a lengthy affair: over the course of a decade, the aristocracy were overthrown and numerous subsequent governments rose up to replace them. The outcome of the Revolution turned France into a democratic republic, while also eliminating the role of religion from its government, making France a secular country which, to this day, remains committed to the separation of Church and State.

However, the French Revolution provides some lasting imagery of social disorder and tyrannical rule, perhaps the sort of thing we can expect to see before, during and maybe even after the End of the World.

Robespierre and the Reign of Terror

Although the French people replaced the monarchy with various political committees – all of which were supposedly equal – Maximilien de Robespierre became the face and representative of a regime which quickly became known as the Reign of Terror.

The government officially embraced terror – or zero tolerance – as a means of control, with the death penalty a regular and swift judgement directed at those who stood against them. While the French people embraced the departure from the established monarchy, this new regime simply replaced poverty with oppression.

Robespierre became the focus for the people's intense hatred and fear. There were several attempts on his life, and Robespierre personally signed a decree that allowed the execution of anyone even suspected of being an enemy of the government. As he exerted an uncomfortable amount of power over the country, Robespierre defended himself against charges of tyranny, even from within his own government.

But Robespierre ultimately fell afoul of his own fears when the military rose up against the government committees, and he was executed without trial for his part in the Reign of Terror. Before he was captured, Robespierre was shot in the face, with the bullet shattering his jaw. Differing accounts suggest this was either a failed attempted suicide or an injury received during the uprising, though it is agreed that he spent the last hours of his life in agony.

Robespierre is an interesting figure, one of the first political villains of the Modern Age and an example of what can happen when power falls into the wrong hands.

Public Execution

The term 'capital' punishment actually comes from the Latin word *caput* – or head – and death by decapitation is one of the most practised classical forms of execution. Capital punishment was not unique to France, but the French Revolution certainly served to reinvent the concept and turn it into something altogether different.

During the French Revolution, the government committees were keen to embrace a new form of execution that could be used for both peasants and nobility: it was necessary that all people be seen to suffer equally in the spirit of *Liberté, égalité, fraternité*.

The guillotine was developed as one such method, a humane means of execution that would be both efficient and final. Other devices similar to the guillotine had been used across Europe for centuries, either strangling their victim or crushing their spine, but the guillotine perfected the art of the blade, leading to a swift, clean death.

What marks this specific form of execution as truly frightening is the spectacle that grew around these public deaths, with a morbid cult of fascination at gathering to watch each usage: programmes were sold listing the names of the condemned; parents would bring their children to warn them to behave; and, surreally, groups of knitting women would become regular features as they fought for the best seats and instigated the most vicious jeers and heckling during the execution.

There are some truly gruesome stories stemming from the usage of the guillotine including the following:

♦ Anna Maria Tussaud was a French artist who became involved in the French Revolution when her wax likenesses of the nobility were used in a protest march some days before the storming of the Bastille. She was later employed to make death masks of the deceased who had been executed. Tussaud lends her name to the well-known chain of waxwork museums, famous for their life-like sculptures.

♦ Charlotte Corday was executed in 1793 for the assassination of Jean-Paul Marat. After she had been beheaded, her head was seized and slapped by an onlooker. Legends tell that Corday was still alive when this happened, responding to the woman who slapped her, even though head and body had already been separated. There are several stories like this, although modern science suggests that these people were indeed dead, with any movement caused by rapidly fading brain activity.

Estimates indicate that over 3,000 people were beheaded during the French Revolution, with the majority of those occurring during the Reign of Terror; the vast majority of these were personally killed by Charles-Henri Sanson, the state executioner.

The Reign of Terror remains a stark warning to any government against turning on its own people, lending much of the imagery that we see in representations of dystopian and post-Apocalyptic governments.

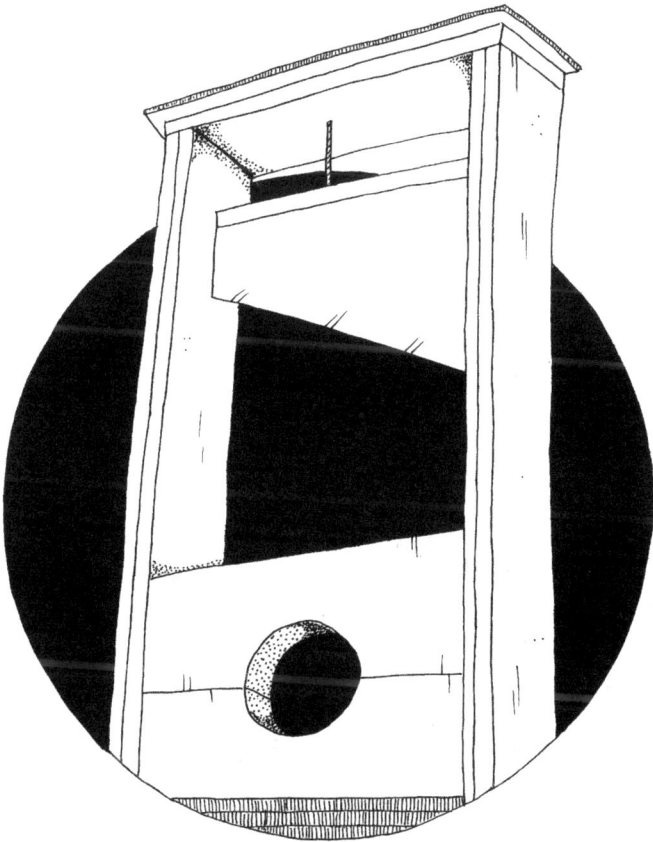

15

APOCALYPSE GOTHIC

THE EIGHTEENTH AND NINETEENTH CENTURIES

If the eighteenth century was a season for political revolution, then the nineteenth century gave us small events that made humanity more aware of our own mortality. Death and destruction became a common theme in works of art, and the increasing improvements toward education and scientific awareness meant that even the common man had an opinion on the End of the World.

One of the common themes running through nineteenth-century thought was in the departure from the religious mode of the End of the World. The groundwork was still there, and the themes remain the same, but in the wake of the Enlightenment and the revolutions of the eighteenth century, writers and philosophers began to look towards science and society for clues on the ultimate fate of humanity.

NEW ENGLAND'S DARK DAY

On 19 May 1780, inhabitants of the east coast of the United States saw an unusual sight in the sky – although they didn't see much that day because the sky had gone completely dark. The phenomenon was witnessed as far north as Maine and extended southwards to New Jersey, leaving a complete blackness in the air that did not clear for twenty-four hours.

Some of the area's more dramatic inhabitants thought that this was a portent for the End of the World; however, students and staff at nearby Harvard University recorded the day's events scientifically, making observations before and after that suggested this was not the Apocalypse – but rather a large forest fire.

CHARLES DARWIN

Prior to the nineteenth century, there was no widely published system on the origin of the species; Charles Darwin's book of that same title changed that thought significantly.

Darwin was not a religious man: although he was raised in a religious community, Darwin questioned his faith as an adult – both as a result of his scientific discoveries and the death of his daughter, an event that he found difficult to reconcile with the existence of any god.

Darwin had no specific thoughts on the End of the World, but he was amongst the first scientists and philosophers to give a legitimate theory and account of where humanity and other species on the planet had come from, in that we have common ancestors with the apes.

Darwin's theories suggested that the concept of a divine creator was nothing more than a story, and that when the world would come to an end, it would not be as a result of these notions.

Most of Darwin's theories have since been proven to be scientifically correct.

MARY SHELLEY'S FRANKENSTEIN

Although it was first published in 1818, when Darwin would have still been studying, there are many similarities in the reasoning between Darwin's work and Mary Shelley's Gothic horror tale.

Frankenstein has been adapted for stage and screen many times and has become a staple of the horror genre. It is often forgotten that Frankenstein is not the name of the book's monster – often referred to as Adam – but rather his creator, Victor Frankenstein. However, Shelley's sympathies are with the inhuman beast, a monstrous creature spurned by a creator who is convinced that he has made an abomination against nature.

Shelley's approach to the subject of creation is explicitly religious, with the creature taking its name from the myth of Adam and Eve: this connotation is not directly referenced in the book, but other phrases and dialogue, alongside Shelley's writings about the book, makes this intention clear.

Shelley's work even draws attention to the pride and hubris of Victor Frankenstein, a man who has stolen the power of creation from the gods: the novel's subtitle of *The Modern Prometheus* calls attention to the classical tale of the Titan that stole fire from the Greek gods and gave it to humanity.

The concept of a creator that has turned his back on his creation is a recurring theme in a lot of religious texts, specifically those drawing on the Old Testament, wondering why God has forsaken his people and allowed them to suffer. If humanity has been forgotten by its God and creator, we are given a terrifying vision of what will happen to those who are forgotten by God during the End of the World.

But Shelley's work goes further and addresses a common theme of the religious Apocalypse: the resurrection of the dead. Shelley suggests that this power no longer lies with God alone, but can be seized by humanity. But, regardless of who is responsible, this will lead to nothing but chaos and fear.

Adam's existence is an interesting conundrum, and some scholars have drawn a line between the monster and Hobbes' *Leviathan*, with the monster standing for a society held together only by the will and creation of one individual.

Although *Frankenstein* is Shelley's best-known book, it is by no means her only contribution to Gothic horror: her 1826 novel *The Last Man* deals with the outbreak of a plague at the end of the twenty-first century, and is one of the earliest examples of this sort of End of the World or post-Apocalyptic literature.

BRAM STOKER'S DRACULA

Although written at the opposite end of the nineteenth century, *Dracula* has entered popular culture in a similar capacity to *Frankenstein*. It operates on as many levels as Shelley's tale, requiring only the slightest scratch beneath the surface to see them.

Published in 1897 by Irish writer Bram Stoker, *Dracula* is commonly read as a struggle to reconcile Eastern and Western philosophies, with the titular vampire representing a superstitious and mythical Eastern tradition that threatens the rational thought – and the women – of modern England. Dracula is also a power that, like Victor Frankenstein, is capable of raising the dead.

The sympathies of *Dracula* lie not with the character himself, but with those that stand against him: they are educated, rational men of repute, representing the legal profession, the aristocracy and the sciences. These learned men are incapable of truly understanding the mythology that Dracula represents, but they are nonetheless successful in defeating him.

This triumph of rational thought is the key to understanding the shifting mindset of humanity during this period: the supernatural was no longer something to be feared. Even though it may not be wholly understood, it was nonetheless something that could be defeated and overcome.

DINOSAURS: THE MONSTERS OF SCIENCE

The nineteenth century also brought its fair share of scientific monsters, perhaps none more terrifying than the dinosaurs.

There are records of dinosaur bones and fossils being discovered throughout history, with the origins of these bones attributed according to local tradition: in China, they were the bones of ancient dragons, while in Europe they were creatures that had died out during the biblical great Flood.

During the nineteenth century, archaeologists and biologists began to look on these bones in a new light. There were similarities between the bones found and those of lizards and reptiles, and the word 'dinosaur' was coined in 1842 by Sir Richard Owen. 'Dinosaur' is a Greek word, literally translated as giant or fearsome lizard.

Based on their size, it was obvious that these dinosaurs weren't some undiscovered species in hiding, but one that had been extinct for many millennia. But this raised another question: what had caused an entire species of that size to become extinct?

FRIEDRICH NIETZSCHE

Born in 1844 in Germany, the philosophy of Friedrich Nietzsche is an integral part of understanding how we react to the End of the World. Nietzsche's philosophies are complex, but where the classical philosophers suggested that all of humanity worked towards an ideal, being intrinsically good, Nietzsche was not quite as idealistic.

Nietzsche's philosophical novel *Thus Spake Zarathustra* is a semi-fictional account of the life of the same philosopher who founded Zoroastrianism. By voicing his own thoughts through this fictional Zoroaster, Nietzsche lends credence to some rather controversial ideas:

♦ Contemporary humanity is in a stage of evolution, moving from our ape-like ancestors towards an existence as the *Ubermensch*, or Supermen.
♦ The future of the *Ubermensch* lay on this Earth: there would be no spiritual redemption or ascension to a higher existence.
♦ There exists a 'will to power' by which all of humanity is being driven towards the possession of power.

A recurring motif and phrase of Nietzsche's work is that 'god is dead': the efforts and purposes of any divinity have little or no bearing on our daily lives. And if any divine being ever did exist, humanity's successes in their own right have proven this god irrelevant: we have become powerful in our own right and no longer need to worship.

Nietzsche's philosophies have a clear and direct influence on some of the politics of the twentieth century and on what society is capable of doing to itself. Like the fallout of the French Revolution, Nietzsche envisions a society that is in danger of descending into chaos.

And in Nietzsche's world, it is humanity who is directly responsible for its own destruction.

16

THE NAZI
APOCALYPSE

THE VÖLKISCH MOVEMENT

Movies like the *Indiana Jones* series have embedded an interesting relationship into our popular consciousness: an association between Nazi Germany and occult practises. But this connection is not limited to Hollywood movies: the Germany of the early twentieth century saw a turnabout in thought and beliefs that harkened back to the older, larger empires that were already dying out.

The nineteenth century saw the rise of a *völkisch* movement in Germany, an embrace of the Romantic ideals of nationalism and classical Germany. Many small movements and organisations sprung up around the country, with the aim of rediscovering this national pride. Although there was no specific goal of recreating an empire, this movement focused on the glory of the Germanic peoples, with their shared cultural and religious history.

Some of these movements embraced a specific *volk* or people, and by linking the nation, and its successes, with a specific bloodline or race, the roots of Aryanism were born.

One of these *völkisch* movements became known as the Thule Society, a Munich-based branch of the *Germanenordern* or Germanic Order. Not only did the Germanic Order embrace the national elements of the *völkisch* movement, but it looked further back in history, claiming power from the country's prehistoric pagan practises. Meetings of the order would gather to read the Eddas and stories of Ragnarok and the Norse gods, with the Thule Society itself named after the missing island of Thule, a Nordic legend about a sunken island in the North Sea, similar to the Atlantis of Mediterranean myth.

By the 1930s, some familiar people had become members of the Thule Society: Rudolf Hess, Hermann Göring, Heinrich Himmler and Adolf Hitler. In the wake of the First World War, the philosophies of the Thule Society moved from culture and religion to more practical ends. The mystical elements of the *völkisch* movement became diluted with racism, anti-Semitism and a resistance to communism, as those involved looked first to close Germany's borders and then to affirm the cultural elements that were part of the nation.

The Thule Society as it stood was dissolved in the 1920s, but not before many of its members had already formed the *Deutsche Arbeitpartei* which would go on to become the NSDAP, or Nazi Party. However, the mythical elements of the Thule Society were not completely forgotten and played a large part in propaganda as the Nazi party preyed on, and made use of, its *völkisch* origins for its own ends.

While not a Germanic symbol, the swastika became intrinsically linked to Nazi Germany. This is a symbol found in many religious, although it is especially prominent in Hinduism. The word swastika is literally translated as 'that which is good for the soul'. The symbol is still used for religious purposes with that meaning.

The symbol was originally adopted by the *Germanenordern*, claiming German historical lineage through some of the oldest cultures in the world. However, the activities of the Nazis led to the symbol being corrupted, and much of the original meaning is lost to modern audiences.

THE HOLOCAUST

As the Nazi party grew in power and popularity, so too did stories about its activities, none of which have proven darker and more disturbing than the Holocaust, the widespread oppression and execution of the Jewish peoples within Germany's borders and beyond. Jews were not the sole focus of the Holocaust, with the Nazis also looking to eliminate homosexuals, the Gypsy community and other ethnic groups.

Some Jewish scholars suggest that the Holocaust was a tragedy that needed to be experienced in order for a greater event to happen, namely the founding of the state of Israel and the call for a subsequent salvation of the Jewish people; others believe that God's absence from intervention in the Holocaust can never truly be understood until well after the End of Days.

Pope Benedict XVI, when he visited Auschwitz, suggested that the Holocaust had been caused by an excess of pride amongst the men and women of the Nazi regime: in killing people of the Jewish faith, they sought to act like God, and take His power for themselves.

There are also schools of thought that suggest that the Holocaust did not happen, or else that its scale and size were significantly smaller than reported. This belief, or Holocaust Denial, typically blames the reports of the Holocaust on a Jewish conspiracy – sometimes even linking it to the New World Order – and suggesting that Zionist organisations have orchestrated events for their own ends. In addition to being a ludicrous conspiracy theory, Holocaust Denial is explicitly a criminal offence throughout most of Europe.

NAZISM AND THE OCCULT

While the racist elements of Nazism have their origins in the *völkisch* movement, there is no known evidence that the Nazi Party was ever involved in any movement to either bring about – or resist – the End of the World. However, there are several semi-religious stories that are worthy of a mention.

The Ahnenerbe

Various works of fiction have called attention to the links between Hitler, the Nazi movement and the various occult and mystical practices that lie in the mythological origins of the Nazi party. Many of these stories focus on the *Ahnenerbe*, a sort of cultural/scientific wing of the *Schutztaffel* or SS.

The *Ahenenerbe* was set up to promote and investigate the concept of Aryan superiority. They conducted various scientific experiments on both Aryan and non-Aryan peoples, and on various excursions throughout Europe recorded instances of pagan beliefs and practises, some of which were then manipulated into pro-Nazi propaganda.

The *Ahenenerbe* are the basis for many of the Nazi villains seen in films like the *Indiana Jones* series, but there is little evidence that they were anything more than a government department that sought to combine science, history and propaganda.

Ravenscroft and the Spear

The Holy Lance is the spear that supposedly pierced the side of Jesus Christ as he was crucified, and writer Trevor Ravenscroft wrote an account of the lance that intertwines the relic with the fate of Adolf Hitler. There are numerous relics that claim to be this spear, and Ravenscroft's account references the Hofburg Lance, currently in Vienna and part of the Austrian Imperial Treasury.

After the German invasion of Austria in 1938, the belongings of the Imperial Treasury were brought to Nuremberg and remained in Nazi possession until the end of the war. Ravenscroft suggests that this spear is possessed by an evil force, which he calls the Antichrist, which exerted some influence on Hitler.

However, Howard Buechner, an American soldier who served during the Second World War, claims that he was contacted after

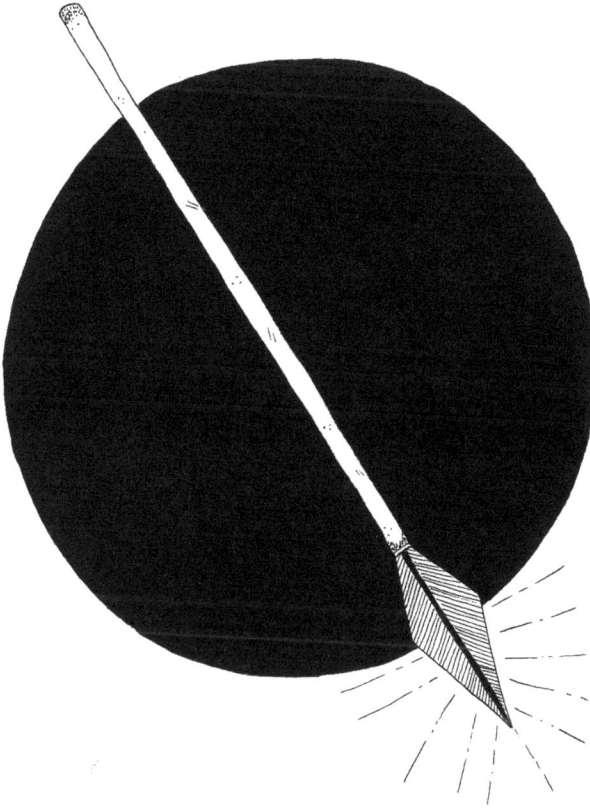

the war by a former U-boat captain who told him that the spear had actually been brought to a secret Nazi base in Antarctica, and the Hofburg Lance is an intricate replica. The real spear was then returned to Europe in the 1970s where it remains in the possession of neo-Nazi forces and continues to have an influence over modern politics.

Hitler as the Antichrist

In contemporary Germany, Hitler was hailed as something of a Messiah, but to the rest of the world his actions were clearly the work of something far more sinister.

Hermann Rauschning wrote a 1939 biography of Hitler called *Hitler Speaks*. The book is largely a fabrication, but paints an interesting image of Hitler waking at night, haunted by demonic spirits and voices.

In her book, *The Externalisation of the Hierarchy*, Alice Bailey suggested that the Second World War was actually the earthly portion of a greater struggle between good and evil, with Hitler, Mussolini and others possessed by dark forces. In this sense, the Antichrist was not one person but multiple people, and with the victory of the Allied Forces, the universe was prepared for the Second Coming.

In a 2006 interview with Vatican Radio, Fr Gabriele Amorth, one of the Vatican's exorcists, claimed that Hitler – as well as Stalin – were possessed by the Devil. He also suggested that Pope Pius XII had attempted to exorcise Hitler from a distance, and that the German leader had remained in his prayers throughout his time as pope. However, Amorth suggests that an exorcism such as this could only have been successful at a shorter distance. As of 2013, Amorth claims to have performed over 160,000 exorcisms – which would average five a day, every day, over ninety years – and has also spoken out about the Satanic dangers of *Harry Potter* and yoga.

THE THIRD REICH

The events of Second World War are well recorded, whether it's the magnetic personality of Adolf Hitler, the nationalist fervour that spread across Europe in the form of fascism or the horrible atrocities committed against various ethnicities and beliefs. However, the Nazi regime does help us to better understand the End of the World.

The concept of the Third Reich was not a uniquely German concept, but had its origins in the religious writings of the twelfth and thirteenth centuries. Gioacchino da Fiore divided human history into three eras:

- the First Age, or Age of the Father, corresponding with the Old Testament;
- the Second Age, or Age of the Son, corresponding to the New Testament and an era when God had sent his son to live amongst humanity;
- the Third Age, or Age of the Holy Spirit, which da Fiore considered was yet to come and would be an era of humanity living with God.

In 1923, Arthur Moeller Van Den Bruck published a book called *Das Dritte Reich*, coining the phrase that we commonly associate with Nazi Germany and turning this Third Age into the Third Reich. Moeller Van Den Bruck applied these three eras to German history, suggesting that the first era had taken place during the Middle Ages, in the form of the Holy Roman Empire; the Second Age had been under the Austro-Hungarian Empire that collapsed in 1918; and the Third Age was yet to come. In some ways, this interpretation was inspired by the five kingdoms discussed in the Book of Daniel.

This idea became twisted under Adolf Hitler and the Nazi regime, who styled the Third Reich as a 1,000-year rule that would bring Germany out of the shadows of the Weimar Republic and restore the country to its earlier glory. In doing so, Hitler portrayed himself as a messianic hero to the German people, but curiously, neither he nor any of his followers made any public claims of divine right or prophecy.

After the Second World War came to a close, the Vatican was encouraged to release a statement condemning the actions of Hitler and his views of a 1,000-year reign. This officially stated that the Millennial reign as discussed in the Bible should be viewed in a spiritual sense, and doing otherwise would not be safe.

17

MUTUALLY-ASSURED DESTRUCTION

If there's a recurring theme throughout the history of the twentieth century, it's that mankind has been on a path to self-destruction. Rather than the End of the World coming from outside of society, or from part of the natural cycle of the planet, we are instead rushing to embrace a man-made Apocalypse. The century has seen two world wars, many smaller skirmishes and world-changing technological advancements.

NOW I AM BECOME DEATH

The mushroom cloud of a nuclear explosion has become synonymous with the End of the World, and one of the men involved in the creation of the nuclear bomb was perfectly aware of the associations between his own work and the End of Days.

J. Robert Oppenheimer was born in 1904 in New York, and studied at Harvard University: he rose through advanced studies quickly, specialising in physics and chemistry and graduating with the highest honours. He continued his studies in Europe and in 1941 was appointed as head of the United States' Manhattan Project to develop an atomic bomb that could be used to bring the Second World War to a close. Oppenheimer was given the title of 'Coordinator of Rapid Rupture'.

Oppenheimer threw himself into his work, recruiting other physicists and scientists; his mixture of skills meant that he was well placed to provide cross-discipline training for those colleagues who needed to better understand the science behind the bomb, turning chemists into physicists and vice versa. The project made its home at the Los Alamos area of New Mexico, and by 1945 the project involved over 6,000 people.

On 16 July 1945, Oppenheimer oversaw the first man-made nuclear explosion and was struck by the beautiful tragedy of the situation.

While many involved in the Manhattan Project regretted that the project had not been completed in time to use against Nazi Germany, they considered its subsequent use in Japan the following

month as an unnecessary show of force to bring to a close a war that they were already winning. Oppenheimer himself travelled to Washington the week after the bombings of Hiroshima and Nagasaki to hand-deliver a letter to the White House, condemning the bombing and calling for nuclear weapons to be outlawed.

Like Newton and da Vinci before him, Oppenheimer's interests went far beyond the world of natural and theoretical sciences, and he turned to Hindu scripture and Apocalyptic imagery to discuss his thoughts on the Manhattan Project, which he felt had hastened the End of the World. He famously stated in a 1965 television interview that he pictured himself in the role of the Hindu god Vishnu, the overseer, transforming into Shiva, the destroyer, at the end of time:

'Now I am become Death, the destroyer of worlds.' I suppose we all thought that, one way or another.

THE COLD WAR

Although the US Army was the first to design and use the atomic bomb, the middle of the twentieth century saw other parties, most notably the USSR, develop their own nuclear programmes, which led to the beginning of the Cold War. Both sides were willing to showcase their weapons in order to instil fear in their enemies, but neither was quite willing to use them, knowing that reprisal would mean certain destruction

The phrase 'cold war' was first coined by George Orwell to describe a struggle where two sides faced each other in the theatre of war, but never actually came into conflict: the outbreak of war would only lead to mutually-assured destruction.

The presence of nuclear weapons created an active threat and a passive deterrent for both the USA and the USSR, as well as many smaller nations that had allied themselves with one force or the other over the period. By the twenty-first century, most nations have condemned the use of nuclear weaponry, or have found less destructive alternatives, although this form of destruction still remains a viable threat.

THE DOOMSDAY CLOCK

Much to the disappointment of many a science fiction fan, the Doomsday Clock is not a real clock: it doesn't even accurately portray time, but is simply a theoretical representation of how close we are to the End of the World.

First referenced in 1947, the Doomsday Clock was created by the University of Chicago's *Bulletin of the Atomic Scientists* magazine and counts down humanity's slow approach towards global disaster, which is represented by midnight.

Over the seven decades since its creation, the clock has moved both forward and backwards, beginning at seven minutes to midnight in 1947. At its closest, the clock was set at two minutes in 1953, with both the USA and USSR testing new nuclear weapons; with the dissolution of the USSR in 1991, the clock was at its furthest setting of seventeen minutes to midnight.

With the end of the Cold War, the doomsday clock has become somewhat forgotten, although an update is still published each year by the University of Chicago. Since 2007, the doomsday clock has also taken global warming into account, leading to a significant jump towards midnight.

The art for the original doomsday clock, as featured on the cover of the 1947 magazine, was designed by Martyl Langsdorf, whose husband worked on the Manhattan Project.

18

ALTERNATIVE BELIEFS OF THE TWENTIETH CENTURY

While the *völkisch* movement arose in Germany, other parts of the world were experiencing their own resurgence of pagan and alternative religions, and the twentieth century saw a significant increase in new expressions of faith that developed and built on existing beliefs.

Some of these beliefs focused on religion: others simply became well-known conspiracy theories that courted the attention of the media and the public alike.

ALEISTER CROWLEY AND THELEMA

Aleister Crowley has become one of the best-known occultists of the nineteenth and twentieth centuries. He formed the Thelemic movement after he claimed to have had an experience with a divine being named Aiwass during a trip to Egypt.

Crowley believed that Aiwass had dictated a new religious book to him, which became known as the Book of the Law, the basis for a new religion that reintroduced the Egyptian gods to the present day. Crowley considered the twentieth century as the Age of Horus, when a new era of thought and morality would be introduced, and he referred to this religion as Thelema.

Thelema does not have a specific theory of how the world might end but uses some of the imagery common to other religions,

including the goddess Babalon, the personification of a divine goddess – she is represented in similar terms to the Whore of Babylon from Revelations.

Crowley was openly involved in two separate secret organisations: the Order of the Temple of the East, itself claiming inspiration from the historical Bavarian Illuminati, and the Hermetic Order of the Golden Dawn, and as with many other secret societies, both of these organisations have become part of conspiracy theories regarding the Apocalypse and the New World Order.

ANTON LAVEY AND
THE CHURCH OF SATAN

Born in Chicago in 1930, LaVey is very much the picture of the modern Satanist with his shaved head, goatee beard and ring-bedecked fingers. LaVey's early life was spent interacting with the arts: he worked as an organist and a psychic investigator, and even claimed to have had a brief affair with a then-unknown Marilyn Monroe.

LaVey had an interest in philosophy and the occult, specifically the imagery that went along with them, and this interest paved the way for the creation of the Church of Satan.

Contrary to the name, LaVey's Church did not revolve around the worship of the forces of evil, but rather the promotion of the self: LaVey responded to Milton's human description of Satan in *Paradise Lost*, a proud man in touch with his own selfish ways. In Satan, LaVey saw a representation of humanity's carnal and base desires that were suppressed by the practises of larger and organised religions.

LaVey also challenged the existence of a God: like Hobbes and Marks, he believed that God was created by humanity as an illusion that provided comfort in the suggestion that there was some benevolent force overseeing a person's life.

LaVey was a popular speaker and released numerous books and albums inspired by his Satanic creed. LaVey, his family and other members of the Church of Satan made many media appearances to distance themselves from the public opinion of ritual abuse and sacrifice, reminding the media that they were not affiliated with dark forces, but rather the human condition.

So great was LaVey's belief in the Church of Satan that his youngest child, born in 1993, even bears the name Satan LaVey.

LaVey's form of Satanism should be considered separately from 'theistic' Satanism, or the worship of Satan as a god or divine figure. This type of Satanism supposedly involved human sacrifice

and ritual abuse, but proof of its existence is found only in theory and accusations. Nevertheless, humanity has responded to this particular form of Satanism, and it was a contributing myth in the persecution of 'witches' and folk medicine and beliefs.

WILLIAM GUY CARR

William Guy Carr served in the Canadian navy during both the First and Second World Wars. When a veteran of two world wars has a theory that a third could be on the way, it makes his argument all the more believable, and Carr became an authoritative conspiracy theorist of the twentieth century.

Carr believed that both of the world wars had been orchestrated to bring about a significant change in worldwide government: the First World War had brought an end to most of the European monarchies, while the Second World War had been caused to construct the victory of Political Zionism over Fascism. Carr foresaw a Third World War involving a conflict between Zionists and Islamic forces, in which both sides would wipe each other out.

Carr believed that these wars were orchestrated by a specific movement that he named the Synagogue of Satan, taken from the Book of Revelations. In fact, Carr suggests that the movement at work in the twentieth century is the same movement as that at work through the Bible, oppressing the faithful at all turns.

Carr provided little basis for proof of his accusations, but his thought processes have proven to be a recurring theme of paranoia and fear aimed at people and beliefs that are not wholly understood.

APOCALYPTIC CULTS: SUICIDE AND DEATH

The latter half of the twentieth century saw widely reported occurrences of mass suicide, many of which had religious and Apocalyptic connotations.

Ritualised suicide is not unique to the twentieth century or the Western world: the Japanese tradition of seppuku involved samurais taking their own life, either because they had dishonoured themselves or were in danger of being caught by an enemy. The practice became well known to the Western world after the kamikaze pilot attacks of the Second World War.

However, the suicide cults of the late-twentieth century had some very different motivators than shame and honour: they specifically saw themselves in relation to the End of the World.

The Order of the Solar Temple

Started in Geneva in 1984 by Joseph Di Mambro and Luc Jouret, the Order of the Solar Temple styled itself on the existence of the Knights Templar, the Rosicrucians and the Priory of Sion. However, the Order of the Solar Temple also had the specific intention of preparing the world for the Second Coming.

The Order spread from Europe to Canada, attracting several high-profile and successful followers, many of whom were happy to financially support the Church. With the End of the World an imminent threat, the Order condoned stock-piling of weapons, arms and provisions as preparations for the Endtimes.

In 1994, Di Mambro supposedly ordered the death of a child that had been born into the Order, claiming that the child was the Antichrist. Rumours suggest that the child was conceived following Di Mambro's infidelity with the child's mother. Several of his followers questioned the order, and Di Mambro began to lose authority over his followers.

On 5 October of the same year, forty-eight bodies were discovered at two separate locations in Switzerland, the result of a mass suicide: twenty-three bodies were found at a secret chamber in Cheiry, with a further twenty-five at Granges-sur-Salvan. Authorities were initially alerted to both scenes after locals reported fires.

All of the bodies were found in similar circumstances, with their heads covered in plastic bags, lying on the ground in a star formation. Many had gunshot wounds, and some had been drugged, although it appeared that all of the deceased had died willingly.

Both sites were rigged with devices intended to burn down the locations, with both Di Mambro and Jouret's bodies found amongst the deceased.

Unfortunately, these were not isolated incidents: shortly after these mass suicides, two further bodies were found in Quebec with ties to the Order; in late 1995 a further sixteen bodies were found in France and in 1997 a further mass suicide took place in Quebec.

Heaven's Gate

The Heaven's Gate cult has its origins in 1972 when Marshall Applewhite was hospitalised and met nurse Bonnie Nettles. The two became fast friends and kindred spirits, in more ways than one. Both abandoned their families, although there was no suggestion that they were a couple: in fact, Applewhite's tastes may have leaned towards a different gender to Ms Nettles.

Applewhite and Nettles both considered themselves to have been enlightened by forces from beyond the Earth. They embraced

New Age spirituality, combining it with religious and scientific concepts to create the Heaven's Gate cult. They believed that the Earth would soon be 'recycled', and that humanity was on the cusp of moving on to the Next Level. This transition would require the cult members to abandon all of their connections to the Earthly realm, including their belongings and physical forms. Applewhite and Nettles suggested that extraterrestrial forces would help on their journey to the Next Level.

When Nettles passed away from cancer, Applewhite claimed that she had already moved on to the Next Level and that she had since returned to visit him, encouraging him to prepare for the next step of the cult's journey.

In March 1997, Applewhite convinced thirty-eight of his followers that the approaching Hale-Bopp comet was the key to their ascension. He was convinced that there was a spaceship travelling behind the comet, and if the cult took their lives, their spirits would be brought aboard the spaceship and to the Next Level.

Applewhite and his followers were discovered dead in a rented mansion in San Diego, their faces draped in purple cloth: all of the cultists had died from ingesting poison, a mix of cyanide and arsenic. One of the Heaven's Gate cult was later named as Thomas Nichols, the brother of actress Nichelle Nichols, Lt Uhura in the 1960s TV series *Star Trek*.

If Hale-Bopp brought any revelations of the Next Level, there are no suggestions that this was experienced anywhere else other than amongst Applewhite's followers.

Jonestown

Although not linked to the End of the World, the phenomenon of suicide cults can't truly be discussed without mentioning the Jonestown mass suicides of 1978.

Born in 1931 in Indiana, Jim Jones was a practicing communist at a time when any such activity was frowned upon in his native USA. Jones formed a Church movement, the Peoples Temple, which participated in faith healing and community outreach programmes in San Francisco; in reality, any 'healing' was just a front for raising money, while Jones' work in the community was a cover for practising socialist ideals in the form of religion.

Facing media and political pressure – following rumours of abuse within the People's Temple – Jones set up a mission in Guyana. The People's Temple relocated to the South American country with several hundred followers, founding a commune and naming it Jonestown.

In 1978, Californian congressman Leo Ryan led a delegation to Jonestown to continue his investigations into the Church. His visit also had a secondary purpose: to reunite some of the Church's members with the families that they had left in the United States.

It's unclear if Jones had misrepresented Jonestown or was making people stay under duress, but during Ryan's visit, several members of the Peoples Temple approached the senator and asked for his assistance to leave Jonestown and return to the USA.

As Ryan, his delegation and the defectors boarded aircraft at the nearby Port Kaituma airstrip, a number of Jonestown security men arrived and fired on the group, killing Ryan and four others. At the same time, Jones spoke to the inhabitants of Jonestown, telling them that Ryan's visit would spell the end of their peaceful community. He urged them to join him in committing 'revolutionary suicide' by ingesting a lethal concoction of drugs.

A total of 909 people died in Jonestown with a further four lives lost at the Temple's offices in Georgetown.

AUM SHINRIKYO

On 20 March 1995, several terrorists affiliated with the doomsday cult Aum Shinrikyo carried out a sarin gas attack on the Tokyo subway, killing thirteen people and injuring up to 6,000.

While initial reports suggested that these attacks were the group's attempt to bring about the Apocalypse, group leaders were adamant that this was an independent attack that, while carried out by group members, was not based on the beliefs of Aum Shinrikyo.

Aum Shinrikyo was formed in 1984 by Shoko Asahara, combining elements of Christianity with New Age practices and a liberal dose of Nostradamus' prophecies. The group believe in the impending start of a Third World War, which will fulfil the biblical prophecy of Armageddon.

Like most conspiracy theorists, the group also believes that Jews, Freemasons and the US government are complicit in the events that will bring about this End of Days.

Aum Shinrikyo has since become known as Aleph. Both incarnations have been recognised as a terrorist organisation by several member states of the United Nations.

CHUCK SMITH AND THE SECOND COMING OF 1981

The Calvary Chapel – not a single Church, but a collection of Churches operating under one banner – was formed in 1968 by American pastor Chuck Smith.

Smith's writings on the End of the World are interesting, even though they have failed to come to pass. Smith mathematically proposed that the 'generation' of 1948 – the same year as the foundation of Israel – would be the last. Suggesting that each of these generations lasts forty years, Smith put forward the theory that the Second Coming would come to pass in 1981, leading to a seven-year tribulation to lead to the End of the World in 1988.

Needless to say, Smith's predicted Second Coming didn't come to pass; it remains to be seen if someone born in 1981 will later lay claim to being the Antichrist or some other figure involved in the End of Days.

JEANE DIXON AND
THE BIRTH OF THE ANTICHRIST

During the 1950s and '60s, American astrologer and psychic Jeane Dixon became a minor celebrity after a number of public predictions – like any psychic, not all of them came true.

Dixon was a contemporary Mystic Meg, complete with a syndicated newspaper column; accounts suggest that both Richard Nixon and Ronald Reagan kept a close, unofficial watch on her predictions via their secretaries and partners.

Dixon appeared to foretell the death of John F. Kennedy, suggesting that the winner of the 1960 presidential election would be assassinated or die in office, but given that this had already happened to seven previous presidents, Dixon's prediction is not as dramatic as it might sound.

However, Dixon did have a clear idea of how the End of the World would come to pass, with her eyes resting on a child who would be born in the Middle East on 5 February 1962. By the end of the century, he would bring humanity together in a new form of Christianity.

Despite the New Age leanings of prophecy and fortune telling, Dixon claimed to be a practising Catholic, and her predictions have been adopted by different Christian Churches with myriad different meanings: while some suggest that Dixon had predicted the Second Coming, others believing that this child would be a false messiah or the Antichrist, who would bring humanity together in resistance.

UFO RELIGIONS

As the worlds of advanced science, philosophy and religion began to grow ever larger, the lines that kept each distinct began to blur.

The twentieth century saw the rise of several 'UFO Religions': some of these religions suggest that humanity was actually created by extraterrestrial forces; others blur the lines between aliens and angels, suggesting that the two may actually be one and the same.

All of these religions have their own interpretations on both the creation and destruction of the world, with many of them building upon adaptations of existing religions: Raëlism goes so far as to suggest that figures like Jesus and Buddha were, in fact, sent by extraterrestrials.

Science is an important element of these religions, with many focusing on a scientific advancement as a means to achieve this enlightenment. Scientology has become a well-known and somewhat notorious UFO religion, as practised by several well-known celebrities, which suggests that the immortal soul, or Thetan, is capable of bringing about great change on the Earth.

THE BIBLE CODE

The concept of hidden messages in the Bible has long been considered, and there are even some references that we can assume to be wholly true, definitive hints and hidden meanings in the book's pages.

However, in his 1997 book *The Bible Code*, Michael Drosnin claims the Bible was written by an extraterrestrial who left these messages with the explicit intention that they be decoded. He also claims that the Bible has predicted other world events, including assassinations and an Apocalypse set to occur in the first few years of the twenty-first century.

Drosnin's claims have met with sceptical analysis from religious and scientific communities due to his seemingly arbitrary methods: some critics even suggest that the same methodology can be used in other books to obtain similarly ominous messages.

LELAND JENSEN

Born in 1914, Leland Jensen was a member of the Bahá'i Church until the death of Church leader Shoghi Effendi in 1957.

Jensen publically backed Mason Remey's claims to be Effendi's successor, thereby ignoring the traditional Bahá'i rules about the appointment of religious leaders. Jensen, along with Remey's other supporters, was excommunicated, and went on to form his own offshoot sect of Bahá'i.

Having spent four years in prison for sexual assault, Jensen was released a changed man and claimed enlightenment over the events that would lead to the End of the World.

He suggested that the year 2000 would see the arrival of God's kingdom, but only after nuclear war had broken out. He also had a specific date for this nuclear holocaust: 29 April 1980.

Jensen oversaw the construction of several fallout shelters, and on the fateful day, led his followers there to wait out the impending disaster. When nuclear Armageddon didn't come to pass, Jensen revised his prophecy and claimed that this was just the start of a seven-year tribulation and test of faith.

By 1987, Jensen had modified his prediction away from nuclear war and suggested that the approaching Halley's Comet would collide with the Earth.

Jensen died in 1996 and never got to see that the world didn't actually end in the year 2000.

THE END OF THE MILLENNIUM

As the year 2000 approached ever closer, many people believed that the End of the World was nigh: much of this belief was simply because a whole 1,000 years had gone by during which humanity had successfully managed to avoid self-destruction.

Many of the religious fears involving the year 2000 revolved around the concept of 1,000 years: with several biblical references to the Millennium, many religious sects feared that the new Millennium could kick-start the Endtimes, with either the Second Coming or arrival of the Antichrist. However, throughout the twentieth century, debate arose as to when exactly the new Millennium would begin: since there is no year 0, this would suggest that any 1,000-year period should run from 1 to 1001. But the current Gregorian calendar has also only been in use since the sixteenth century, rendering both arguments invalid for the most part.

Most of these fears were unfounded: the year 2000 – and 2001 – seemed to roll in and out without the world ending.

However, in the lead-up to the Millennium, a new technological threat emerged that we learned to know and love as the Millennium Bug, or Y2K. The problem of Y2K arose because of the convention used in computer programs where two digits identified the year –

meaning 1990 would be written as '90' and so on. This could have created a problem for the year 2000, with certain programs refusing to recognise the year '00' and others becoming convinced that they had actually travelled 99 years back in time.

The Millennium Bug presented a number of terrifying situations in which the computers responsible for missile launches and defence satellites might have experienced issues.

Interestingly, the Millennium Bug was not a unique problem and was preceded by a far more likely issue on 9 September 1999, since '9999' is used by many computer programs as reference to an unknown date.

Most of these issues were easily fixed by upgrading systems to include a 'century' option, with many companies and organisations setting up specific taskforces to ensure that IT departments were prepared for any crises that might emerge. There were only a few small issues reported from the year 2000, and it seemed like the world would survive for another 1,000 years.

19

APOCALYPSE NOW

THE TWENTY-FIRST CENTURY

Although we're still in the relatively early days of the twenty-first century, there have already been a few close shaves when it comes to the End of the World, or events that might mark its approach. The twenty-first century has brought us international warfare, scientific experiments to recreate the Big Bang and an act of terrorism that would change the face of international politics forever.

11 SEPTEMBER 2001

Anyone over a certain age clearly remembers the events of 11 September 2001 where three separate planes crashed into US landmarks, bringing down the World Trade Center and damaging the Pentagon. The events of that day, the lead-up to it and its aftermath have been discussed many times since, and are probably too recent to discuss with the same broad hindsight as some other historical events in this book.

The terrorist attacks of 9/11 led to intensive commentary on international politics and the role of religion and politics in the End of the World. With the attacks carried out by fundamentalist

Muslims, racial tensions in the USA rose to an uncomfortable high and remain incredibly complicated. Blame for the attacks was levelled at Osama bin Laden, rumoured to be orchestrating an al-Qaeda terrorist empire from Afghanistan: even as the world joined in mourning with the USA, all eyes were focused on the Middle East.

Although more information has been revealed about the terrorist attacks, there are still many conspiracy theories, including suggestions that the US government was aware of the planned attacks and allowed them to happen to urge political and military action in the Middle East, or that the attacks were orchestrated by the New World Order/Illuminati in an attempt to kick off a Third World War.

After the events of 9/11, pastor and political commentator Jerry Falwell appeared on *The 700 Club*, a popular Christian TV talk show. He suggested that the attacks had been caused by the absence of God in daily American life, and he blamed 'pagans, abortionists, feminists, gays and lesbians' – amongst others – for having allowed the attacks to happen. Falwell later apologised for his comments, but he was not the only pastor to suggest that, even in the twenty-first century, punishment from God was something to fear.

THE PREDICTIONS OF PAT ROBERTSON

Jerry Falwell's statements were made in conversation with broadcaster and conservative Christian Pat Robertson, who is no stranger to controversy. Although Robertson partly retired from media appearances shortly after 9/11, he continued to remain an active voice with comments and opinions on world events.

On numerous occasions, Robertson has suggested that natural disasters have been sent by God to clear away unclean communities or as punishment for accepting sin – usually in the form of pre-marital sex, same-sex relationships or non-Christian beliefs. He became so well known for these controversial opinions that some are even falsely attributed to him, as occurred in the wake of Hurricane Katrina.

These views are in keeping with the Old Testament depictions of God and His divine punishment, with Robertson claiming that these 'sins' will bring around the End of Days.

Robertson made several predictions of other global events, typically with regards to natural disasters or American elections. In 1976, Robertson predicted that the world would end by 1982 and he supported this prediction on numerous TV broadcasts.

In 1991, he published his own book titled *The New World Order* and discussed the Satan-led global conspiracy to bring about the End of Days. It still hasn't happened yet.

GOG AND MAGOG AT WORK

The political and economic fallout from 9/11 was not confined to America: the rest of the world felt the repercussions of that day's events, although where the USA experienced anger, most of the rest of the world was consumed by horror and sympathy.

As American politicians surged towards revenge and retribution, an interesting story came to light when world leaders discussed the events of 9/11 in the context of the End of the World, using language explicitly derived from the Book of Revelations. As this story unfolds, it serves to highlight some of the significant differences between fears and beliefs about the End of the World on both sides of the Atlantic.

George W. Bush, in his effort to gain support for military action in the Middle East, urged European leaders to act since 'Gog and Magog were at work' in the area. The phrasing says much about Bush's fears and the reaction to 9/11 from a certain type of American mentality. However, Bush's language was somewhat inappropriate for his European equivalents.

In fact, Bush's biblical reference was so alien to French president Jacques Chirac that Chirac and his aides had to consult with biblical scholars and eschatologists at the University of Lausanne.

These scholars provided some contextual explanations for Chirac and his cabinet, raising highly sceptical questions about the usage of such prophecies in the modern world.

Thomas Römer, professor of theology at the University of Lausanne, called any biblical references 'uncertain and unclear' and would later retell the story of his involvement in a 2007 edition of the University's magazine, *Allez savoir!*

SEARCHING FOR THE BIG BANG: THE HIGGS-BOSON

In 1964, a group of physicists including Tom Kibble, Gerald Guralnik, C.R. Hagen, Francois Englert, Robert Brout and Peter Higgs formulated a theory for the existence of a new sort of particle. These particles were a necessary part of the standard model of understanding for particle physics but, without proof of their existence, they were just assumed to exist, with the rest of the model taking shape around this question mark.

While the existence of this particle was theorised for thirty years, it only entered public awareness with the publication of *The God Particle* in 1993, published by Leon Lederman and Dick Teresi. As a popular science book, *The God Particle* attempted to explain how or why the existence of this particle would affect the world and help physicists to better understand primal forces. The name of the book was meant as a tongue-in-cheek joke, but nonetheless was adopted by many media outlets as a byword for the particle and the search for it.

This nickname earned these experiments some notoriety over the next two decades, not least due to the construction of the 27km-long Large Hadron Collider (LHC). Not only was this an impressive feat of engineering that involved over 10,000 scientists and engineers, but the size, scope and very nature of the experiments that would take place at the location led some people to believe that the Large Hadron Collider would create an explosion that would lead to some Apocalyptic scenario.

To discover the Higgs-Boson particle, two other particles were accelerated through the LHC and collided, with the resultant impact creating new and diverse particles that had never been observed before. As befitting amateur scientists and media reporting, the words 'accelerator' and 'collision' led many people to believe that the scientists at CERN (The European Organization for Nuclear Research) were attempting to recreate the Big Bang.

After some initial teething difficulties, the Large Hadron Collider was up and running in 2008. By 4 July 2012, CERN had discovered their first new particle, which was later confirmed to possess the properties expected of the Higgs-Boson. The world didn't end, but it's interesting to note that even in the twenty-first century, people can still fear scientific endeavours.

CERN isn't all about *Top Gear*-style scientific experiments of making particles go really fast and crashing them into each other: we also have it to thank for the existence of the Internet. The first 'World Wide Web' was created by Tim Berners-Lee as a program called ENQUIRE, initially used by the several thousand employees of CERN as a means of sharing information between different departments and projects.

HAROLD CAMPING

Pat Robertson is not the only American minister to predict the End of the World through the twentieth and twenty-first centuries: in fact, Harold Camping's predictions became much better known and reported on – and ridiculed – throughout the world. Part of the widespread knowledge of Camping's predictions was due to his high-profile radio show, and the large amount of monetary support that he received from followers to help publicise his predictions.

Camping's initial prediction for the End of the World was 1994, in a book surprisingly called *1994?* Befitting the question mark in the book's title, Camping also provided 2011 as an alternative date, and when the Apocalypse failed to happen in 1994, this became the accepted date for Camping's prediction.

Like many other eschatologists, Camping's predictions were based on close readings of different Bible passages, including application of 'code' where the passage in question was not to be taken at face value. Camping gave two specific dates for his Apocalypse: the Rapture would happen on 21 May with massive earthquakes, with the End of the World occurring exactly five months later on 21 October.

Camping was unavailable to the media for comment when the Rapture failed to happen on 21 May 2011, and on 22 May

he released a statement outlining his disappointment, including the revision that the Rapture would occur at the same time as the Apocalypse in October.

In June, Camping suffered a stroke, and gradually retired from the public eye in advance of 21 October.

However, when 21 October came and went with no Apocalypse, it appeared that Camping had learned the error of his ways: unlike his predecessors' habits of consistently revising their predictions, Camping suggested that his attempts to set a date for the Apocalypse were sinful and contravened a specific passage of the Bible, indicating that no man will know the hour of the Endtimes.

Camping returned to closer readings of the Bible, but refused to be drawn on further predictions: instead, he wished to better understand the Bible and its messages and purpose. Camping passed away on 15 December 2013, ultimately never seeing the Rapture that he had expected.

In September 2011, both Camping and Pat Robertson were awarded an Ig Nobel Prize, a parody of the well-known Nobel prizes. They were given the award specifically for their contribution in teaching the rest of the world to be careful when making mathematical assumptions.

A.J. MILLER AND THE DIVINE TRUTH

In the early part of the twenty-first century, Australian A.J. Miller claimed to come to the realisation that he is, in fact, the reincarnated Jesus Christ; adding further weight to his claims, Miller's partner Mary Suzanne Luck claims to be the reincarnated Mary Magdalene.

Miller has moved on from his old life as an IT specialist and founded a retreat in Queensland where he openly teaches. Miller believes that Jesus' original teachings have been corrupted since he first taught on Earth, and that he is now teaching and rediscovering the 'Divine Truth'.

Although Miller has been preaching since 2003, news outlets have only recently begun to pay attention to his teachings. Not all of the coverage has been favourable: some have likened Miller's behaviour to that of the cult leaders we've looked at already. Miller has faced his criticism with good humour, even braving the cynical *This Morning* couch in 2013.

It remains to be seen if Miller's status will give way to the apocalyptic Second Coming and what role he might play in the pending Enditmes.

2012

While the Mayans get the blame for suggesting that the world would end in 2012, there is little evidence to suggest that they truly believed this: rather, 2012 brought an end to a significantly long cycle, or 'long count', of the Mesoamerican calendar.

Some people assumed that this 'long count' meant that the Mayans had been divinely inspired, possessing some secret knowledge for the coming Apocalypse, albeit thousands of years in advance of it occurring. In fact, the Mayans did claim that the calendar and their knowledge of it was a gift from the god Itzamna, but they did not claim to know when the world would end.

The Mesoamerican long count calendar measured seasons with a high degree of accuracy unseen in similar cultures of the time: this calendar records dates in a lengthy format, with reference to days, seasons of the sun and moon and also *tun* (360 days), *k'atun* (20 *tuns* or 7200 days) and a *b'ak'tun* (20 *k'atuns* or 144,000 days.) As the name suggested, the calendar is constructed to be used over a long period: as it works in cycles of 20, the calendar actually resets every couple of thousand years.

The most recent *b'ak'tun* ended on 21 December 2012, resetting the calendar to the same format it had around 5,000 years ago.

The Mayans and other Mesoamerican tribes did not attribute any special meaning to this date or any others although, like modern humans, they celebrated the end of every cycle and the start of the next.

Instead, the concept of a 2012 Apocalypse has its origins in the New Age movement of the mid-twentieth century, with many writers discussing the Mesoamerican calendar and other theories without fully understanding them, and seeing connections that may have just been coincidental.

Most of the writers who discussed these Apocalypse theories are well noted for their beliefs in aliens and usage of psychotropic 'mind-expanding' drugs; in comparison, most scholars of both Mayan culture and eschatology dismissed the theories of a 2012 Apocalypse as nonsense. But that still did not prevent the date receiving widespread media coverage.

THE ZOMBIE CANNIBAL APOCALYPSE OF 2012

A phrase thrown around in a primarily fictional context, the zombie apocalypse is exactly what it sounds like. Zombies have proven to be a popular enemy in TV, comics and movies through the end of the twentieth century. We've already seen how the resurrection of the dead is an important part of the End of the World for many religions; the concept of a zombie apocalypse suggests that these revenants might be more interested in eating our brains and guts than living with us in peace.

The *zombi* is referenced as part of West African voodoo (or *vodou*) and other places where it is practised, including Haiti. The *zombi* in this case is a corpse that has been brought back to life by a *bokor*

– or priest/sorcerer – to serve as a slave. There are several records of these *zombis*, by both native writers and visitors: the former highlight the mystical nature of the *zombi*, stressing the power and fear of the *bokor*, while visitors suggested that these *zombis* were actually patients who had been treated with psychotropic drugs and were left susceptible to suggestion and manipulation.

The image of the zombie as an undead creature feeding on flesh is mostly derived from George Romero, whose 1968 film *Night of the Living Dead* was amongst the first to portray our current image of this particular branch of the undead. This image has become enduringly popular, and most Hollywood zombies either neglect or outright ignore their voodoo origins in favour of portraying a world where human survivors struggle with each other in a planet overrun by undead fiends.

However, that doesn't stop some recent news stories from using the word 'zombie' with abandon and suggesting that this breed of zombie isn't too far removed from real life.

The Miami Zombie

On 26 May 2012, Rudy Eugene (31) assaulted a homeless man named Ronald Poppo (65) in a particularly vicious attack. Most of the attack was recorded on Miami traffic cameras, and authorities have since used these to recreate a fuller picture of the day's events.

After experiencing car trouble, Eugene left his car and proceeded to walk the rest of his journey. During his walk, Eugene stripped completely naked. When he encountered Poppo on the side of the street, Eugene proceeded to attack him, removing Poppo's trousers and then biting off parts of his face. Poppo survived and his later testimony suggests that during the attack, Eugene plucked out his eyeballs.

One of the most terrifying elements of this attack lies in Eugene's reaction: upon the arrival of police officers at the scene, Eugene ignored their demands that he stop, and instead growled at them. He was shot five times before the attack was brought to a close, with eyewitnesses suggesting that he shook off the initial bullets.

Reports from Poppo and the attending officer, Jose Ramirez, suggested that Eugene was acting as if on drugs, although blood tests after his death found only marijuana in his system. However, toxicologists working on the case were quick to point out that the drugs industry is advancing at a quicker rate than tests can keep up.

While multiple news outlets reported this story with the word 'zombie', it is, unfortunately, not unique in its gruesome content.

May 2012 saw a number of similar attacks around the world, with several blogs and Internet sites linking the events and painting a picture of an impending zombie apocalypse:

♦ Pornographic actor Luka Magnotta posted a video online, implied to be part of a horror movie. The footage showed the brutal murder of a naked man, with some of his flesh consumed in the process. The video was reported to the site's owners, and when police investigated, they linked this video to the murder of Chinese student Jin Lun, whose body parts had since been mailed to various Canadian state departments. Magnotta was subsequently arrested in an Internet café in Germany, whilst reading news reports about his own crime.

♦ In Hackensack, New Jersey, police responded to a 911 call and found themselves confronting a knife-wielding Wayne Carter. Carter reportedly stabbed himself multiple times, cutting himself open and revealing his intestines. Carter then proceeded to throw his skin and intestines at the arresting officers.

♦ In Maryland, Ghanaian exchange student Kujoe Bonsafo Agyei-Kodie was staying with the Kinyua family pending extradition after his visa had expired. The Kinyua's 21-year-old son Anthony was also staying with them after being released on bail following an attack in his college dorms. Agyei-Kodie was reported missing on 25 May, with police calling to the home after Anthony's brother found organs stored in the house's basement, leading to Anthony's subsequent arrest and incarceration.

Although these events paint a chilling picture of the United States in May 2012, there are other stories from the twenty-first century that are similar in content and brutality. In a well-publicised case from Germany in 2001, Armin Meiwes was charged with the murder and cannibalistic consumption of Bernd Jürgen Armando Brandes. The incident was covered internationally, with several headlines focusing on the fact that Meiwes had recruited Brandes as a willing victim via a personal advert, with Brandes participating in the process.

THE KILLER ANIMALS OF 2013

The year 2013 saw a spate of animal attacks that were reported throughout the world, many of which had deadly consequences, even taking the form of quasi-biblical plagues.

Russian Zombie Birds

In August 2013, residents of Moscow began to notice some unusual behaviour amongst the city's feathered inhabitants and concerns were raised about the significant increase in the number of dead and dying pigeons, many of which dropping from the sky. Those that were still living ignored nearby humans, walking around in circles or standing on their heads.

The pigeons were given the nickname of 'zombie pigeons' in local and foreign media. Some newspapers and media outlets even suggested that these events signalled the beginning of the Endtimes, pointing towards a prophecy by Russian mystic Gregori Rasptuin. Unfortunately, most of these newspapers only point towards each other as a source, with none actually referencing this questionable prediction directly.

Local veterinarians, meanwhile, insist that these pigeons were just suffering from a particularly bad bout of salmonella poisoning, and that mass animal deaths are a regular occurrence.

Attack of the Killer Giant Hornets

After rapid urbanisation and a particularly humid summer in northern China, June 2013 saw a series of aggressive attacks of a specific type of hornet that was a lot bigger and scarier than you might think.

The Asian giant hornet is native to the area, clocking in at a terrifyingly impressive 2.5cm in length, with a stinger that accounts for nearly 0.5cm. The breed is known locally as 'yak killer hornets', given their size and the considerable amounts of poison they carry in their sting. These monstrous creatures accounted for over 2,000 attacks over a short period of time, and at least forty of these cases resulted in death, many of which were caused by an allergic reaction to the hornet's venom.

Curse of the Spiders

Hornets weren't the only creatures out to poison us in the summer of 2013, and there were a number of attacks a lot closer to home and by something that looks a lot more innocent. However, these cases might justify that arachnophobia you've always had.

A humid summer was once again to blame when a particular family of spider became commonplace around the British countryside: these large creepy-crawlies are similar in size and shape to the deadly black widow, earning themselves the nickname 'false widows'. While these spiders aren't deadly, they still got blamed for deaths and injuries to household pets, labourers and children; in the finest tradition of tabloid journalism, those same newspapers also ran stories involving concerned parents terrified to allow their children out to play.

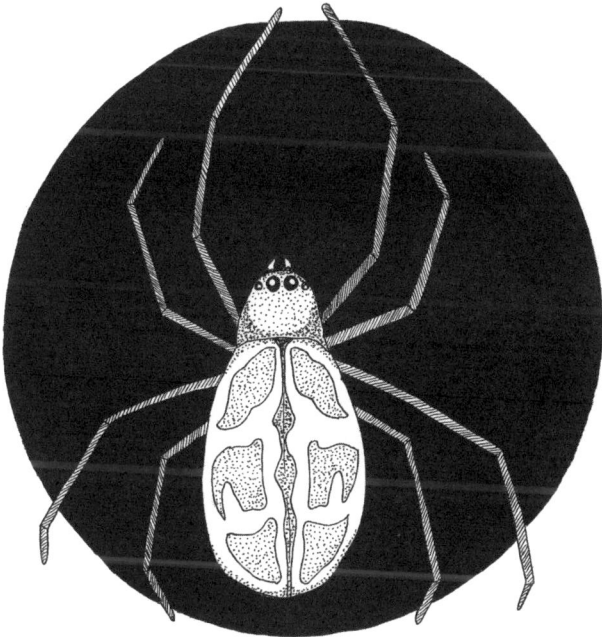

PART 4

APOCALYPSES YET TO COME

As we've seen throughout this book, there are many different forms and shapes that the Apocalypse could take, from an immediate event that causes the destruction of the entire planet to a literal slow burn that might spell certain death at some stage in the future.

As we come to the end of our journey, we'll look at just some of these events, as well as some hints that might even help you survive when the Four Horsemen come knocking.

20

A BEGINNER'S GUIDE TO SURVIVING THE APOCALYPSE

The survivalist movement has its origins in the post-nuclear world of the 1950s: having seen what the nuclear bomb could do in Japan, the world waited with bated breath for all-out nuclear war to begin. But this prolonged waiting didn't appeal to everyone's tastes. Survivalists, or preppers, prepared for the potential Apocalypse with bomb shelters and food stores, learning basic survival skills and teaching them to their families.

Several generations later, survivalism has become a way of life for thousands of people, many of whom have been raised and taught by parents and grandparents. Not all preppers focus on the ultimate end of the Apocalypse, however. Survivalism means being prepared for electrical outages, earthquakes, floods and other natural disasters, all the while being prepared to be entirely self-sustaining should the need arise.

WHAT TO PREP FOR

There are plenty of things that we take for granted in the modern world that form the basic foundations of survivalism: food, water and healthcare are obviously at the top of the list. Survivalism is a personal practice, and as such, there are many different types of preppers: some place a practical emphasis on what they are preparing for, like natural disasters or civil disobedience. For others, survivalism is just one outlet for a greater paranoia about zombies of the biblical Endtimes.

When it comes to survivalism, even the most over-the-top fears should not be discounted, with many preppers suggesting that having a small item and not needing it is preferable to going without when this is an important requirement. You should prepare for what could be the worst-case scenario in such a way that you are still comfortable when this scenario doesn't come to pass.

There are several different levels of preparedness practiced by survivalists, and the chances of survival increase significantly with each level: estimates suggest that people with zero preparation would survive no more than a week, while the ultimate prepper – one who is prepared to be entirely self-sufficient – could go 'off-the-grid' and survive for upwards of three years.

THE FOUR BASIC NEEDS

There are four key requirements necessary for prepping (to some, these are self-explanatory, but in keeping with the nature of prepping, one should always be prepared, even if that means re-stating knowledge you already know):

◆	shelter	◆	water
◆	fire	◆	food

These are basic human needs recognised by all survivalists, from the boy scouts through the military and up to the most hardened prepper. All of these are, of course, nothing without a basic understanding of your environment and first aid.

Shelter
One of the most basic human requirements, the need for shelter varies depending on your location: for urban dwellers, this could

be as simple as ensuring that your home is sturdy and kitted accordingly; for those in a rural environment, this could involve finding or constructing a shelter, whether out of natural materials, finding a suitable cave or even carrying a tent with you.

This requirement becomes all the more important in cases of extreme weather. If the End of the World involves ice, fire or water, that proves all the more dangerous for the prepper: extreme weather could kill you within three minutes if you are not prepared.

Of course, the type of shelter required depends on the type of Apocalypse you're experiencing, and the sign of a successful prepper is one who is prepared for both that erupting volcano and the next ice age.

Fire

Your stomach might not agree, but fire and warmth are more important to your survival than food or water. Of course, the need for fire is once again dependent on your environment and what sort of shelter you have, but a warm locale doesn't mean you won't need fire: remember, you still need to cook and ward off those hunting animals.

Being truly prepared for the End of the World means that you know how to build and start a fire from foraged materials. So no matter how shiny your Zippo lighter is, you should still be well versed in rubbing two sticks together.

Water

The average human probably wouldn't survive any longer than three days without fresh water, and the prepper should be prepared to source water from wherever possible, as well as dealing with the possibility that traditional water sources may be contaminated.

Some survivalists will stock up on bottled water, others on tablets that will purify water, and then there are those that are fully prepared to drink their own urine. Unfortunately, with water ranking so highly as a basic need, you can't always be picky about where you get it from.

Food

After putting a roof over your head, warming your toes and filling up your glass, only then should you look after your appetite: the fact that you can survive longer without food than anything else means that those cravings will just have to wait.

Some preppers deal with the need for food by stocking up on canned and non-perishable food, and that's obviously a lot easier to deal with for survivalists who intend staying in their own home. However, for those without the luxury of an extensive basement, the wilderness survivalist should also be capable of identifying and foraging for edible vegetation, and maybe even playing amateur butcher.

SHOULD I STAY OR SHOULD I GO?

So the End of the World has happened, and you weren't one of the lucky ones to get raptured. What do you do?

Survivalists differ on what the first thing you should do is, and most of that difference depends on where they are located. Some suggest heading into the wilderness or some other location – bugging out – while others suggest that you stay where you are and make your own location secure. As you can probably guess, this practice is called bugging in.

Bugging-out necessitates you having a bug-out-bag, a small bag with some of your necessary survival tools: you should also have a pre-decided location to go to, perhaps somewhere where food is in abundance or shelter will be easy to come by.

Bugging-in is decidedly easier, but carries with it a whole other bunch of challenges: staying in or near your own home means that you know your own surroundings and you're likely to already be aware of any threats in the area. But bugging-in, especially in an urban area, means that food will possibly be less easy to come by over a long period of time.

And then, there are the neighbours.

Obviously, bugging-in has the added bonus of your neighbours nearby, people that you should be able to depend on and club together with for shared protection. But as we all know, the threat from other people can be just as bad as the threat of the Apocalypse itself.

MUST-HAVE SUPPLIES

In no particular order, here are just some of the things you should have in your bug-out-bag or somewhere safe in your home.

- water
- map of the local area
- a small axe or other tool for cutting wood
- fire-starting equipment – fuel, lighter
- first-aid kit
- non-perishable food
- weapons/tools
- sleeping bag/insulation
- clothing/footwear suitable for climate and exposure
- torch
- cash
- compass
- ID
- rope

All these supplies vary, depending on just where you intend going when you need to tap into these survivalist skills, and perhaps some will be rendered completely useless if it truly is the Apocalypse. But a good survivalist is one who can get multiple uses out of one item, something to bear in mind when preparing your own kit.

PLANNING FOR THE FUTURE: ORGANISATIONAL SURVIVALISM

Mormons believe that each member of the Church should prepare for adversity by having a three-month stockpile of food and drinking water should it be needed. This has only recently been revised downwards from six months.

Several UFO religions claim to have access to advanced technology, and rumours persist that they are researching cloning and other things that will enhance the human lifespan. While not 'survivalism' in its strictest sense, the principles of avoiding death and prolonging life remain the same.

The Norwegian government, with global consent, have developed the Svalbard Global Seed Vault, an installation 120m deep within a mountain complex, complete with hi-tech security measures. The vault is a measure to ensure that various forms of plant life will survive the Apocalypse – albeit in certain forms. There are over half a million different species stored in the Svalbard Seed Vault, with similar plant-based programmes existing at the Royal Botanical Gardens in Kew. San Diego Zoo also cryogenically freezes animal matter in a similar scheme to preserve life.

So when the Apocalypse comes, and you're desperate to reboot the agricultural industry, you know to hitchhike your way to Norway, Kew or San Diego.

21

THE ULTIMATE FUTURE

What sort of book about the End of the World would this be if we didn't close by looking ahead at some of the things we should still be scared of? We can scoff all we like at our ancestors and their fear of random dates, but now you can prove yourself better than all your friends by picking an equally random date in the future and telling them just why the world won't end then.

CLASH OF THE PLANETS

As we discover more and more about the planet on which we live, we're also significantly more comfortable with the volatile ecosystem around us. Volcanoes, floods and extreme weather conditions can still lead to significant loss of life, but for the most part, they can be predicted and resisted: they are no longer the Apocalyptic affairs they once were, certainly not Apocalypse-with-a-capital-A.

And so, humanity has begun to look further afield for threats to our humble civilisation.

In the late twentieth century, Wisconsin-based Nancy Leider claimed to have been visited by a race of aliens called zetas who warned her of several cataclysms that would befall the planet Earth. This would begin with the arrival of 'Planet X', a gigantic planetary body that would pass so close to the Earth that it would stop the planet's rotation for a period of five days and then reverse the Earth's magnetic poles.

Leider first claimed that Planet X would arrive in 2003, and that the approach of the Hale-Bopp comet was a precursor to Planet X's arrival.

When this failed to transpire, she revealed that this initial date was a test to see how corrupt authorities would react: they had confirmed her suspicions by ignoring the threat, therefore confirming the purpose of the 2003 date. After this reaction, Leider refused to disclose the actual predicted date.

Planet X has since been adopted by other UFO-religions and cults, and its arrival was one of the many suggested events that could occur in 2012.

Leider's claims of the existence of Planet X coincides with Zecharia Sitchin's theory of the planet Nibiru, a twelfth planet in the solar system whose orbit intersects with Earth's every 3600 years. Nibiru is a twelfth planet because Sitchin claims that it was previously responsible for the destruction of other planets in the solar system, two of which have become the asteroid field between Mars and Jupiter.

Sitchin claimed that Nibiru is inhabited by a race of aliens who were responsible for the creation of humanity: their power and abilities led to them being worshipped as gods, and the long cycle of Nibiru's orbit explains both the absence of gods in the modern world and the myths shared by many religions about their return.

However, Sitchin's 2007 book, *The End of Days*, suggested that Nibiru would not cross paths with Earth's orbit until the year AD 2900, thus distancing himself and his theories from the far more immediate Planet X.

2017: THE SWORD OF GOD BROTHERHOOD

After the not-at-all-near-miss of 2012, many news sources reported that the date for the Apocalypse had been revised to 1 January 2017. Rumours were that this date had been revealed to the mysterious Sword of God Brotherhood by the Angel Gabriel himself.

Now comes the tricky part: there are no reputable sources proving the existence of the Sword of God Brotherhood, or even where these reports of 2017 came from.

Some sources suggest that this organisation is an offshoot of The Covenant, The Sword and the Arm of the Lord, a survivalist movement shut down in the 1980s, and there is a striking similarity in the names of both organisations but, beyond that, the Sword of God Brotherhood remains an enigma.

2035: ALIEN ANGELS

Nibiru and Planet X are not the only potential Apocalypses to face us that involve extraterrestrials: the UFO religion Raëlism suggests that a second coming will take place in 2035, but that this will not be a coming of gods but rather a race of aliens called Elohim.

The Elohim are somewhat like angels and Raëlians are quick to point out that they should not be treated as gods: rather, they will return to welcome humanity into the wider universal community. The Elohim have already made their presence and mission known to various prophets – namely the religious leaders of the last few thousand years.

The arrival of the Elohim will mark a significant shift in civilisation: perhaps it won't be the End of the World, but it will be the end of the world as we know it.

2050: TECHNOLOGICAL SINGULARITY

While no specific date is given for humanity to achieve technological singularity, most futurists and writers agree that this is likely to occur in the middle of the twenty-first century, and various parts of the entertainment media have jumped on that bandwagon.

This isn't just some random date: these writers have looked at the developments of technology over the last few decades and traced its potential growth and progress into the future.

Put very simply, technological singularity is the ultimate *Terminator* scenario, but movie fans will be disappointed to hear that it hopefully doesn't involve time travel or a naked Arnold Schwarzenegger.

Instead, singularity is the creation of a computerised intelligence that exceeds that of humanity. While the aforementioned *Terminator* implies that this technology might turn on humanity, writers suggest that technological singularity will simply trigger a shift in society that will significantly change civilisation. Unfortunately, there are no real predictions as to just what we'll do when we're armed with hyper-intelligent computers.

2100: MALTHUSIAN CATASTROPHE

In 1798, economist and cleric Thomas Malthus wrote that the Earth was having difficulty keeping up with population demands. Malthus foresaw a time when the planet would no longer be able to provide for its substantial human population, and throughout the twentieth century it looked as if this Malthusian Catastrophe was imminent, with the population expected to reach 8 billion in the early twenty-first century.

However, these concerns appear to be somewhat unfounded, as countries around the world gradually go through a 'demographic transition', finding a balance between high and low birth rates, quality and length of life and access to contraception.

As population levels stabilise, some economists expect that they will actually start to decline before humanity reaches a size where it is too large to support itself. Whether the planet's natural resources continue to support us that long remains to be seen.

600 MILLION – 4.5 BILLION: SOLAR DEATH

The sun is currently about halfway through its life cycle, and still capable of supporting life on this planet for another couple of million years. That's certainly long enough for you and your family to survive for the next couple of generations.

But as with all balls of flaming chemicals, there's a chance it will turn on us. And that time is likely to come in around 600 million years.

As this time approaches, the composition of the Earth's atmosphere will change dramatically – it's changing right now, but in subtle ways that probably won't affect us during our lifetimes. Eventually, the Earth's atmosphere will contain too much carbon dioxide to effectively support plant life, that important thing at the very bottom of the food chain, and we could end up going the same way as the dinosaurs.

After a further billion years, the surface temperature of the Earth will have increased significantly to affect the oceans, leading approximately half of the world's water to evaporate into the atmosphere and turning the planet's surface into a dry, desert wasteland.

By 8 billion years' time, the sun will have expanded and probably swallowed Mercury and Venus, with Earth next in the firing line. There are different theories as to how badly Earth will be affected by this: some physicists and astronomers suggest that the Earth will be just outside of the sun's gravitational pull and will survive in some form, while others reckon that the Earth will be swallowed just like the other planets.

Regardless of the planet's fate, the best-case scenario is that the surface will be reduced to seas of molten lava. But we can draw some comfort in knowing that, by this period, all life will be long extinct

3 BILLION YEARS: GALACTIC COLLISION

Earth, the solar system and most of the stars that we look at each night currently exist in the Milky Way galaxy, with our nearest neighbour being the Andromeda galaxy. Scientists have suspected that both galaxies are drawing together and will eventually merge: in 2012, after years of studying both galaxies' interactions through the Hubble telescope, we were finally given proof.

The Milky Way and the Andromeda galaxies are moving closer together at a rate of approximately 120km a second. In about 3 billion years, the two galaxies will collide and merge into a super-galaxy.

There are no clear theories on just how this will affect a planet as small as Earth, especially since we'll all be long-dead by then anyway. But it's likely that any galactic collision will massively affect gravity throughout both galaxies, and therefore the placement of the sun and any of its remaining surrounding planets.

10 TRILLION YEARS: THE BIG FREEZE AND THE BIG CRUNCH

There are currently two different theories about the ultimate fate of the universe, and both depend on what will happen as the universe continues to expand.

If there is no force to resist the ongoing expansion, the universe will continue to expand unhindered and, in around 10 trillion years' time, the fundamentals of the universe will have started to decay as they move so far apart that they can no longer interact: matter and gravity will fail until the universe gets progressively emptier.

However, if there is an external force operating on our universe, or if the conditions are just right, the universe could start to contract, pushing all remaining matter closer together, and significantly increasing all of the gravitational forces at work. As matter is forced together, multiple black holes will form, which will then compress into a massive black hole. Again, if the conditions are right, this could trigger a massive build-up of energy, causing another Big Bang and resulting in a reboot of the universe.

Perhaps the world itself could be resurrected from the dead and survive another day, before the next universe's version of Earth and its inhabitants go through it all over again.

Visit our website and discover thousands of other History Press books.

www.thehistorypress.co.uk

The History Press